Francis Lieber

A

POPULAR ESSAY

ON

SUBJECTS OF PENAL LAW

AND ON

UNINTERRUPTED SOLITARY CONFINEMENT

AT

LABOR

AS

CONTRADISTINGUISHED TO SOLITARY CONFINEMENT
AT NIGHT AND JOINT LABOR BY DAY
IN A LETTER TO JOHN BACON

Elibron Classics
www.elibron.com

Elibron Classics series.

ISBN 0-543-97932-6 (paperback)
ISBN 0-543-97931-8 (hardcover)

This Elibron Classics Replica Edition is an unabridged facsimile of the edition published in 1838 by the Philadelphia Prison Society, Philadelphia.

A

POPULAR ESSAY

ON

SUBJECTS OF PENAL LAW,

AND ON

UNINTERRUPTED SOLITARY CONFINEMENT

AT

LABOR,

AS CONTRADISTINGUISHED

TO

SOLITARY CONFINEMENT AT NIGHT

AND

JOINT LABOR BY DAY,

IN

A LETTER

TO

JOHN BACON, ESQUIRE.

PRESIDENT OF THE PHILADELPHIA SOCIETY FOR ALLEVIATING THE MISERIES OF PUBLIC PRISONS.

BY FRANCIS LIEBER,

CORRESPONDING MEMBER OF THE SOCIETY; PROFESSOR OF HISTORY IN SOUTH CAROLINA COLLEGE.

Mild Laws—Firm Judges—Calm Punishments.

PHILADELPHIA:

PUBLISHED BY ORDER OF THE SOCIETY.

1838.

E. G. DORSEY, PRINTER,
LIBRARY STREET.

Since the Philadelphia Prison Society has done me the honor of voting the publication of the following pages, I would state, for the more professional reader, that the present Letter may be considered as a forerunner of a systematic work on punition. A most important subject belonging to penal matters—punishment itself—has not yet been treated upon a firm, comprehensive and scientific plan, or as an independent science. Yet there exist many valuable materials; the literature on several subjects, which would be comprised within its province is considerable, and the discussions on punishment have arrived at a degree of maturity, as well as assumed an importance to all civilized nations, that it appears to be high time to concentrate and digest all that lies before us or has been discovered, into a consistent and strict system, which, like every true science, should endeavor to establish the essential principles peculiar to its subject matter, and to deduce from them sound laws. It is proposed to call this science penology, which will necessarily treat of punition theoretically, practically and historically; of its relation to the political community as well as to the psychologic state of the offender. In the present essay I was obliged to touch on subjects belonging to the province of penal law proper, and on others appertaining to penology. I trust the essay itself will show the necessity of a combination which might have been inadmissible in a strictly scientific work.

I ask for no favour at the hands of the reader; the subject alone can engage us; but I claim as a right that he who shall begin the perusal of the following pages at all, should fairly read them to the end, and not judge by skipping, still less by garbled extracts. The subject is too grave, the essay resembles too much the few outlines of a sketch, to allow of an indulgence which may remain harmless if the object of the work is mere entertainment, though it must ever be a trying one for the writer.

THE AUTHOR.

Dear Sir,

A few years ago I had the honor of addressing a Letter on the relation between education and crime, to the venerable gentleman who then filled the chair, which you now so worthily occupy—to Bishop White, a minister whose zeal never made him a zealot; who sought the essence of religion in peace and not in excitement, and who, through an unusually long life, preached with ardor and proved by deed that charity and good will toward all, are the chief precepts of the christian religion toward our fellow men. He is no more; but let his memory be among us, by looking upon him as an example of kindness, when we have to defend a cause which we consider sacred, against imputations and attacks not always bearing the appearance of having originated only from a want of sufficient acquaintance with the subject-matter. Let me endeavor to speak of the cause alone, and not think of the persons that are for or against it.

Partial friends believe that those remarks have not remained altogether without some good effect here and abroad, where charges of a grave kind against the belief that education strongly tends to diminish crime, were to be rebutted. Perhaps it was in consequence of this kind view of my labour that my friends proposed to me, when lately at the North, to write an exposition of the advantages resulting from the Pennsylvania system,* as we believe experience has fully proved what, on

* Common name for the system founded upon uninterrupted confinement at labor.

philanthropic grounds we ardently hoped, and in expecting which the knowledge of man's character in general seems to warrant us. I consider the cause too important not to have yielded at once, well knowing that subjects which affect mankind so deeply and at large, are best promoted if every one cheerfully contributes his mite, however well he may be aware that there are others whose labors would be more efficient. Every individual has his views and his own experience, a faithful statement of which cannot but have a beneficial tendency, though the degree in which it promotes the cause may be but moderate. Besides, I have lately visited again some of the most important penitentiaries on the two different plans, have had my conversations with their superintendents, and made my inquiries of their inmates: I believe, therefore, that my few remarks may not prove altogether useless. Long ere this should I have accomplished the desire of my friends had not professional and literary labours rendered it almost impossible. Nor is it unlikely that I should have delayed the labor for some weeks longer, had I not lately received the Twelfth Annual Report of the Boston Prison Discipline Society, which does not only show the same spirit of hostility to the Pennsylvania system that has characterized, I believe, every number in the series of these annual reports, but contains remarks of so surprising a kind, that I resolved forthwith to take up the pen. It may be objected indeed, why pay any special attention to remarks the very character of which, it would appear, must greatly deprive them of their effect, while the world at large seem agreed, or daily becoming more so, that uninterrupted solitary confinement at labor is the preferable, because the most humane, yet most effective mode, to which society can resort in punishing its unfortunate members; as we see it at home from the increased number of penitentiaries on the Pennsylvania plan, and abroad, from the reports made on the American penitentiary system, by gentlemen selected for this task, by their respective governments, and who are unanimous in favor of our system? Why are you not satisfied, it may be asked, with so impartial a statement as that lately made by Mr.

Julius, in his Letter to Mr. Crawford, (Leipzig, 1837,) which must be cheering to all friends of the Pennsylvania system?* The answer is: Because our subject is not an historical fact, which, once clearly established, may be left at rest. We have to do with a cause in which millions and millions, individually and collectively, are interested, bodily and morally, and though all the world should have penitentiaries on the Pennsylvania plan, and but one single prison on a different one should remain, and men should persuade the people not to change it, it would be worth our labor to answer the arguments and to endeavor to induce the people to change their penitentiary, as soon as circumstances may permit: for there are living men involved in the question; suffering men; more or less guilty men, some of whom may yet be rescued: generations of convicts yet unborn are in question, who, like most of their predecessors, shall begin with apparently trifling offences when young, and at a stage of life and criminality, when they yet may be brought back to the paths of order, loyalty, industry, morality and worth—generations that in turn shall become parents, and upon whom the moral issue of their offspring will depend again.

The remarks in the Twelfth Report of the Boston P. D. Society, to which I chiefly alluded, are to be found on page 59, and relate to the new penitentiary at Columbus, Ohio. They run thus:

"The deaths in this institution, the last year, including the two cases of suicide mentioned above, out of 290 prisoners,

* PRISONS ON THE PENNSYLVANIA SYSTEM IN THE UNITED STATES.

Philadelphia—Eastern State Penitentiary.
County Prison, Moyamensing.
Pittsburgh—Western State Penitentiary.
County Prison, Allegheny county.
Jefferson, Missouri—State Prison.
Trenton, N. J.—State Prison.
Newark, N. J.—Essex county—Built, but not occupied.
Providence, R. I.—State Prison—Building.
City of New York.—House of Detention—Built.

were 11, or about 4 per cent., which is a very unfavorable bill of mortality. How much of this is owing to doing violence to the nature of man, in keeping him shut up in a solitary cell on the Sabbath, and not suffering him to come forth and enjoy the soothing and healing influences of the Sabbath school, the sanctuary, and the public worship of Almighty God, no man can tell. The solitary cell of a prison is a deadly place to put a man in to spend his Sabbaths. Legislators of Ohio,—ye fathers, ye brothers, ye sons,—will you place *men*, sustaining these relations, week after week, month after month, and year after year, in solitary cells to spend their Sabbaths? Will you place mothers, sisters, daughters, in solitary cells to spend their Sabbaths? Will you do it? If you will, may the Almighty avert from you the dreadful affliction of having members of your own families placed in these circumstances! May you never know, by your own experience, what it is! May you never be driven to suicide by it! May you never have your flesh and blood dried up by the slow and consuming effects of unmitigated solitude and despair!"

I shall have to touch on the charges, implied in these lines, which seem written with so much emphasis; and therefore dismiss for the present this repetition of charges, long ago proved to be false, leaving it in the meantime to their writer, to show how it is doing violence to the nature of man when he is shut up on sabbath; and to the good Ohio legislators, how they will take the courteous compliment paid them by the allusion to the possibility that they themselves or their wives and children may one of these days be locked up as criminals. I turn at once to the subject.

The inquiry as to the first course from which we derive the punitory power of the state is not a merely curious one. Whatever view we may take with regard to it, will necessarily influence our procedure in punishing; it will widen or contract the limits we assign to penal authority. In some countries, as in England and the United States, the jurists have but superficially occupied themselves with the true foundation of the right we have to punish, and the real end we have in view in punishing; a necessary consequence of which has been, that no fixed standard of punishment has ever been established, and punishments of excessive cruelty as well as others showing a morbid philanthropy, are found with the same race, and at the same time in curious contradiction to each other. The German, French, and most Italian jurists have, with great zeal, and not unfrequently with much shrewdness and close reasoning, inquired into the origin of all penal right, but they have again greatly neglected the practical operation of the various systems.* None of the parties have paid sufficient attention to the psychologic part of penal law, treating the whole matter, not only the principles, as a general one, without sufficient reference, and a thorough scientific inquiry into the nevertheless close relation which must ever exist between punishment and the given state of civilization, on the one hand, or to the psychologic state of the criminal himself on the other. I do not hesitate in confessing that the part of the fourth volume of Blackstone's Commentaries, which treats of punishments, has ever appeared to me as one of the least successful passages in that classical work, however useful some remarks of his were for the time, when Romilly had not yet directed public attention to the injudicious cruelty of many barbarous laws in the code of Britain. Chancellor Kent, than whom no author has better and more justly succeeded in establishing himself far and wide over a vast country as authority in one of the gravest causes of mankind—the administration of justice—during his lifetime, and to whom I feel the deepest gratitude both as a citizen of the United States and individually, for the indulgent views he has been pleased to take of my humble labors—glides still more briefly over this subject, which has perplexed for so many centuries the ablest philosophers and inquirers into the dearest interests of society, from Aristotle to Kant, from Kant down to the latest times.

* The French, of late, may be mentioned as making an exception to the last remark.

The present letter is of course not the proper place to examine all the theories that have been given with regard to this subject, or to establish a new one; more room and arguments of deeper penetration than a popular essay allow, would be required; yet, in order to know which is the best and most legitimate mode of punishment, we must needs know what object we have in view when we punish, and whence we derive our right to inflict punishment, which, if ascertained, will show us, at the same time, how far we may go in punishing. For this purpose I may be permitted briefly to review a few of the most prominent theories, and to indicate the one I may have arrived at.

Common sense has long acknowledged that punishments are necessary, and that society has a right to punish; or, in other words, practical life has long produced the most perfect conviction in all men, the criminals by no means excepted, that a political society cannot exist without punishment; which conviction agrees with man's moral consciousness and conceptions, according to which, evil ought to be the consequence of bad, and the enjoyment of some good, the consequence of good deeds. But common sense is very far from having settled whence we derive the right of civil punition, what are its due limits, and for what precise purpose we punish; else we should not find the great variety of punishments, many of which we cannot explain on the ground that they were called for by the different degree of civilization existing with those to whom the punishment was to be applied, or by the fact that these various punitory modes were or are calculated for different classes; for instance, for soldiers, sailors, serfs, freemen or noblemen. We meet in history and the present times, with fine, confiscation of property, apology, privation of honor and stamping infamy on the culprit, degradation, ridicule, public exposure on the wooden horse, the drunkard's cloak, the fiddle, whirligig, brand, stocks and pillory, the ducking stool, flogging, singeing the soles, running the gauntlet, the picket, bastinado, banishment, transportation, imprisonment, lying on edged laths, flaying, maiming, branding, boring the tongue, blinding, racking, killing in almost all possible ways, by strangulation, poisoning, beheading, throwing from a precipice, burning, exposure to wild animals, quartering, breaking on the wheel, stoning, crucifying, pressing to death, burying alive, chaining to beasts of the forests, drowning, starvation, sawing in two, walling up, eating alive (as the Battas do to this day), condemning to suicide, with the choice by what means the malefactor shall think fit, selling into slavery, stamping the children and children's children of the culprit with infamy. Every species of punishment here mentioned, which admits of any variety at all, has been made use of in almost infinite variation, while this melancholy catalogue is far from being complete. It is evident that this great diversity cannot spring from the difference of the society alone, as I have said already, or the difference of the crime to be punished, but must be accounted for, in a very great degree, by the different views which have been taken, both of the ultimate object of all punishment, and its psychologic operation on the individual to be punished, as well as the society which it was calculated to affect, by way of example.

Of the various grounds which have been assumed in order to find a firm basis for the right or obligation which a political society has to punish offenders against its laws, I shall examine here the following:

1. *Expiation.*—If we mean by expiation, a suffering for a committed wrong, solely because it is a wrong, an offence against some law—in short an atonement, without any view as to repairing an injury or improving the sufferer—an absolute suffering for a wrong considered absolutely, it is either an act of a purely moral character, or, if the view be taken that it is useless suffering, a revengeful act; in either case it affords no ground for civil punishment. If expiation be taken in the sense we have given, it would found the right of punishment solely in the offence; but the offence, as such, is something past, not any longer existing, and, therefore, something entirely removed beyond the sphere of the state of political action. Seneca has already said: "No wise man punishes because wrong has been committed, but that none may be committed; for it

is impossible to revoke the past, but the future may be prevented." Expiation, I said, is a purely moral action, and thus belongs to the forum of conscience alone. Political expiation would be infliction of suffering without object—cruelty; for I know of no other definition of cruelty than that it is the inflicting of suffering for no end, or for a bad one.

2. *Necessity, Expediency.*—The assumption of this ground seeks for the right of punishment in the very opposite to the previous one—in the effect of the punishment alone, entirely passing over the offender, the individual to be punished—in short, it affords no right of punishment, and destroys all marks of distinction between punishment, and acts of bare necessity which produce any degree of suffering in others; e. g. as was the case when, lately, part of the crew belonging to the unfortunate ship Medusa, resolved to throw overboard all who could not work the frail rafts from which salvation alone could be expected, and yet were consuming the scanty provision. Expediency alone, can never afford us a standard of the application of suffering, or we might soon arrive at the resolution to kill all patients in a time of a contagious disease. Blackstone's instance of the inefficiency of all laws respecting the injury done to public roads by wagoners, and yet the want of a right to punish the latter with death, (even though it should be believed that this punishment would prevent the evil,) is here in point. When pope Sixtus V. was enthroned, the states of the church swarmed with banditti. He made the communities answerable for the crimes which the robbers should commit in them; made the kinsmen of robbers pay the reward offered for the heads of the latter; pardoned and rewarded with money, and a pardon for some more friends, any robber who would bring the head of a companion; visited with death any opposition to the police, and said: "as long as I live, each criminal must die." Thirty robbers had fortified themselves near Urbino. Mules laden with poisoned flour, were purposely driven past them, robbed, as was expected, and the brigands died.*

* Ranke's Popes, their Church and State in the 16th and 17th centuries, Vol. I.

All this may have been expedient, necessary if you choose, but is it punishment? It is chains, war, or whatever else it may be called, but not civil punishment. In short, we are but too well aware that the prevention of crime alone, neither affords a right, nor a relation between the degree of punishment and the character of the offence, which our whole moral character nevertheless urges us to establish, and at the want of which we feel morally offended—feel, that there is something out of joint in the state machine, which ought to be repaired.

3. *Deterring*, establishing examples, the prevention of criminal action in some, by exhibiting to them the suffering which it has brought upon others. This theory is but a species of the above, and fails entirely to furnish us with a *right* of punishing. For, though it may be granted that some are deterred, by the sight of suffering, being the effect of crime, it does not prove that we have a right to use another person for this purpose. The theory is essentially immoral. Man is a moral being, and the first moral law is: "Make in no case whatever of another moral being a *mere* instrument for your own purpose." Being a moral being, means having a distinct moral value of his own, which excludes the idea that others can make a mere instrument of this being. This, however, would be the case if we punish; that is, if we cause one human being to suffer solely for the benefit of others. We must first acquire the right of punishing. Here again the theory does not give us a just standard of punishment; for if the legislator were convinced that the people would not allow themselves to be deterred from a certain crime, whatever the punishment might be, because its cause was too deeply rooted, beyond his reach, as is by no means unfrequently the case, he would be bound not to punish the crime at all, however atrocious it might be; for the only object of punishment being to deter others, this failing, the whole punishment becomes useless. On the other hand, he would be bound to affix the severest penalty to the slightest act of pilfering, if he were convinced that without this severity the people would not be deterred, because surrounded by too much temptation, e. g. by inviting orchards

in autumn. In fact, the theory of deterring would necessarily lead to an inverse ratio of punishment from what our whole moral nature prompts us to expect: atrocious crimes, because rare, and because fewer people are ready to commit them, would demand less deterring, i. e. punishing, than the stealing of wood in the forests; for when the winters are severe, you cannot prevent the poor from obtaining it, whether it belongs to them or not.

4. *Special prevention.*—Some distinguished lawyers have seen the moral and practical difficulty of the last mentioned theory, and have substituted the theory of special prevention, which is simply this: the offender has shown that he is dangerous to society; or, in other words, disturbs its lawful state; punishment, therefore, is inflicted to prevent him for the future from doing so, either by deterring him, or by obviating the possibility of injury, either by taking away his personal liberty for life, or life itself. Again, we have no firm basis; for, according to this theory, it would undoubtedly be but to kill at once every offender, or to leave unpunished every one who committed an offence which, in its nature, cannot be repeated; for instance, a man who beats his wife most cruelly: the wife dies. He has never beaten or offended any one else: shall he go at large? Besides, what we look for, the source of the penal right, is not furnished us by this theory. In Dutch Guiana and the French West India colonies there existed formerly a law that a runaway slave should have one of his legs chopped off. This was certainly effective special prevention: was it just? was it right?

5. *Warning.*—The theory of warning is argued thus: The state has the undoubted right and obligation of protecting itself and maintaining its lawful order. Every member is a being capable of disturbing it. The state has therefore the right to warn every being capable of disturbing it not to do so, by affixing beforehand, a penalty to every offence. The state, in doing so, injures no one, for it inflicts no evil, and prohibits nothing but wrong. Warning, however, would be useless and but empty sound were the penalty affixed to each offence be-

forehand not actually imposed, in each case of actual transgression. This theory has a high degree of plausibility, and I own that I had myself arrived at it, in reflecting upon this momentous subject, when at a later period I found it had been carried out by one of the most distinguished criminalists of the age, Mr. Feuerbach, the penal lawgiver of Bavaria. Some of his followers have much developed his fundamental idea. Still, this theory is founded upon that fallacy called begging the question; for when we are asked to grant the truth, that the state has a right to warn its citizens, we either understand by warning, simply and strictly warning, or warning with the right of executing the threatened penalty in case of contravention. If we mean the first, we grant nothing, and no right of punishment can be deduced from our concession; if we mean the second, we grant the very thing to be proved, namely, the right of punishing. It is likewise deficient on the same point on which we have found the others so defective; namely, it affords us no standard of punishment. The state might warn by affixing the penalty of death to the offence of picking up a valuable article in the street, without endeavoring to ascertain its owner; and though it would be indifferent to all who should never thus offend, what penalty was affixed, it would still be of the greatest importance to the offender when the warning comes to be executed.

6. *Contract.*—The state, it is said, is founded upon a contract; each member enjoys its protection on condition to conform to its laws, and cannot complain if that evil is inflicted which, according to these laws, therefore, according to the contract, is known to be stipulated for the offence or breaking of the contract. This theory is invalidated by two objections. First, the state is not founded upon a contract, as I have endeavored to show in a work now revising for the press.* For the present purpose it is quite sufficient to ask what sort of a contract that can possibly be, in which I had never a part, or from which I can never withdraw myself, and according to

* Political Ethics.

which I am nevertheless exposed to many very severe sufferings. Ask a convict whether he has ever made a contract to be punished should he offend, and if this contract is a mere fiction it is altogether insufficient to afford a ground upon which we can build the right of a matter of so grave reality as punishment. Secondly, if the contract were granted, we have not yet proved the right which the contracting powers had of making it. Beccaria founding his argument against punishment of death on the theory of contract, says that no man can be supposed to grant away conditionally his life, nor would it be lawful, because the right of life is inalienable. Equally inalienable is the right of personal liberty, of volition, of locomotion, if I offend not, thereby, others, so that confinement would be as inadmissible as capital punishment.

7. *Correction, Reform.*—Philanthropically disposed persons have asserted that the only legitimate object of punishment, and, therefore, the only ground on which we can found the right of punishing, is the correction or reform of the convict. The reform of the convict, be it moral or political, that is, only as to his habits of obedience to the laws, from whatever cause he may feel induced to obey, enters largely into every true penal theory, as I shall show presently; but it is far from affording us the right of punishment, aggravation, or the object of penalties. The reasons are:

a. On theoretic grounds.

b. On practical grounds.

As to the first, it is sufficient to remember the fundamental idea of the state, the very principle on which it is founded; in justice, right, and on general grounds, the state has nothing to do with the moral correction of the citizens. If this were granted as a subject for legitimate action of the state, the most insufferable inquisitorial power would be at once established, and, in spite of all political activity, the endeavors of the state would still remain fruitless. We cannot, therefore, assume correction as the original ground of a penal right, but we shall see, that the state can acquire it over certain individuals, if the right of punition is once established.

If we assume correction or reform as the basis of all penal right, two things are clear at once. First, we must allow those criminals to go free, a reform of whom, according to all experience in different countries, cannot be expected; men who have spent a long life in pilfering, stealing and other transgressions to which low, mean and dirty habits are required rather than unbridled passions, and who are generally styled inveterate or incorrigible rogues. For to punish them without object, would be senseless, or, as I have observed above, cruel. On the other hand, we should be obliged to leave untried and unpunished any individual, of whom we are well satisfied that he heartily repents his offence and will never offend again, as cases of the kind occur for instance when murder has been committed in passion excited by unusual provocation, and the very enormity of the act warrants, according to the whole previous life of the offender, that its deep impression upon his mind will prevent any recurrence. Secondly, in conformity to this theory it would be necessary, in general, to inflict a much more impressive punishment, or longer confinement, on those offenders, who, though their offences be comparatively slight, have contracted a habit of offending, than on those convicts who have greatly offended, but not from habit; in short, we should be obliged, ordinarily, to punish the thief more severely than the murderer. At least in this country, and I believe, in most other civilized societies, in which private property forms one of the most distinctive features, it has been found that, in general, the offenders against persons show themselves more reclaimable than offenders against property; while the girl, who begins with prostitution and pilfering, is hardly ever reclaimed, though she may never go, in her offences, beyond the line drawn by these two transgressions. All the intelligent wardens of our penitentiaries, I believe, are agreed with me on this point; and the reason is clear. Those individuals who offend against property, do so, in most cases from neglected education and a consequent vicious life, in which the sensual part of our nature has acquired a decided preponderance, and reason, with her regulating power, has become depressed, the intellect weakened, and all ethical notions disjointed and obliterated. Those, however, who offend against persons, do so, in a great many cases, from temporary impulses; at the time they committed their act, reason, indeed, was obscured, and had no power over them; but the whole moral character need not on that account have become diseased. Vital ethical power enough may have been left to restore the individual, with the assistance of a judicious moral physician, to a state of ethical health.

As to the practical objections against this theory, it suffices to mention, that in nearly all cases, it is next to impossible to ascertain, with any degree of satisfactory certainty, whether real reform has taken place, or merely deception. This deception is not always hypocritical; the convict frequently deceives himself, and takes a temporary state of feeling for a thorough regeneration which will prove firm against new temptations. Convicts have frequently spoken to me on this point, with great candor. "If," said they, "I would be sure that I should feel, when at liberty, as I do now, I know I should be a good man, but it is so difficult!" This theory, founded solely on correction, has, indeed, misled some writers so far as to maintain, that the convict should be released the moment he has reformed; an extravagant and monstrous idea. Besides the radical error of this assertion, which is but one of the many thousand errors, produced by the confusion of the family relations, essentially founded upon affection and forbearance, with the political, essentially founded upon justice and right, the inevitable and almost sole effect would be the engendering of the rankest hypocrisy on a most extensive scale. Correction, then, is not the sole object of civil punition as it is of domestic, nor the original ground from which we derive the penal right vested in the state.

8. *Retaliation.*—Retaliation as the sole basis and object of punishment, admits of nearly the same objections to which expiation is liable, with this difference only, that it becomes the more objectionable the more it approaches to revenge; for there is very little difference, if any, between revenge and the

producing of suffering, privation, pain, or whatever may constitute the punishment, for no other purpose than because suffering or injury has been produced first. The state cannot revenge itself; there is no organ in the state which has the capability of revenge; and if, nevertheless, individuals, clothed with the authority of the state, do revenge themselves, they act personally and criminally, not politically and publicly. The state is an institution founded on justice, for protection and the attainment of the highest objects of man, who can obtain them only in society, in which alone he can, according to his nature, unfold his entire *humanity;* revenge, however, is personal; it is the satisfaction of a feeling of wrong produced in us, by causing, in turn, some suffering in him who made us suffer. Retaliation alone and revenge, as the object of punishment, belong to those early stages of society, when the state has not yet clearly severed itself from the family, and personal wrongs are taken to be family wrongs; when the moral nature of man is active indeed, for it is always so in some mode of manifestation or other, but when offences are not yet viewed in any different light than private offences, and revenge is the only or prominent effect which the moral feeling of wrong or injury produces as yet in the injured party. The history of penal law with all nations begins with private revenge of individuals, or the families or tribes to which they belong. It passes over into atoning expiation (*compositiones*). The next step is, that a judge awards these compositions, or, if it cannot be paid, hands over the offender to revenge. This forms the transition to the civil punishments proper; for at all times man has felt, that wrong ought to be punished.

There is a species of revenge which may be fitly mentioned here in a few words. No one can read the penal codes of most nations, without discovering that some passages which provide a punishment altogether disproportionate to the offence, would have been complete only if the words: "For how hast thou dared to disobey my authority" had been added. That forgery was punished in England until of late with death, arose, I grant, from a belief in the general danger to which the country would be exposed, should any more lenient punishment be substituted. The case of the Rev. Dr. Dodd, who was executed in 1777, for forgery, sufficiently proves it, when the monarch was most anxious to exercise his prerogative of pardoning, and yet obliged to yield to the public fear of danger. But when we find in many codes death as the punishment for making or wittingly circulating false coin, we must acknowledge, that neither the danger either in the degree of the facility with which the crime can be committed, or which may accrue from it to society, nor the difficulty of detection, nor the immorality of the act itself, warrants this degree of severity. It is the idea of offended majesty which dictates so disproportionate a punishment, and what else is this than revenge, or something very near it? Let us, in this case, however, not rashly exclaim at tyranny, wilful oppression, &c. What father is there among my readers who, having faithfully searched his heart, will not admit, that very frequently when he has punished his own child, the chief agent in his mind was the prevailing indignation at the disobedience of the child, the opposition it had thus offered to his commands, and not the wrong, as such, which the child had done? Authority, wherever it may be lodged, is displeased at opposition, not only because it is opposition, but because the opposition leads to evils. This species of hidden revenge in state matters appears to me to be the latest remnant of that mode of redressing wrongs which is solely founded upon revenge.

9. *Retribution.*—Many philosophers, and among them some of the most distinguished, saw the objections which could be made against the penal systems which derived the right of punishment from the object or intended effect of the punishment itself, and, therefore, said that civil punition—by which, it will have been observed, I mean all punishment administered by public authorities, as contradistinguished from domestic or merely disciplinary punition—is inflicted for the sake of justice, and no other reason. Offence must meet with evil as its effect; it is a postulate of reason: punishment is actual retribution, i. e. the absolutely necessary effect and consequence of

the offence: crime, the contradiction to the rightful order of things which reason demands to see realized in the state, must be extinguished, annulled, blotted out, and the means of effecting this is the punishment, which thus, as I have said, becomes essentially retribution—political visitation as it were. Justice is considered in this case as something absolute, existing for itself, or an organic thing which, being counteracted by something, counteracts in turn, to re-establish itself in pristine or rather absolute purity as first founded and conceived in reason. To use a comparison, punishment is the process by which the curative power of nature ejects the poison of disease, or, if another simile be preferred, punishment is the negative quantity requisite to defeat and reduce to zero the quantity crime. But how does punishment obliterate the offence? I cannot see it. Does it do so in the abstract, ideally? The offence is ever a distinct and concrete one, a fact alone for the state. The theory rests upon the confusion of sin and crime or state offence. Sin is wrong inasmuch as it counteracts and disturbs the moral order of things. It belongs to the conscience and its God to judge of it; the state cannot have cognisance of anything but the fact, and how can a fact be obliterated? A thorough refutation of this theory which, nevertheless, as most of the others, leads to a partially correct view, if carefully treated would require a different range of argumentation from those allowed in the present lines. May it suffice here to observe that it does not, in spite of its positiveness, dispense with the question why? and wherefore? For in all matters of right, law, and politics, I can acknowledge but one axiom, namely: "I am a man, therefore I have a right to be a man." All the rest must be shown how, why, on what ground, for what purpose? It is right if the penal code of Charles V.* uses the expression: "for the love of justice" shall a man be punished; but if we omit to show why, justice becomes a sort of Moloch, which demands with absoluteness his sacrifices. It has ever appeared to me that, granting this absolute foundation of civil punition,

* Article 104.

it would be easy, consistently to show that all offences are alike, however this might at first glance militate with a view of retribution, because they have their characteristic trait of offence in the fact that they contravene the absolute demand of reason, in what degree, matters little; nay, a degree of offence is hardly possible, and the first unlawful act committed by a youth of the age of discretion ought to be visited with the same punishment which is inflicted upon the most hardened criminal. The practical effect of this theory has been, that its adherents have exerted their mind to solve the question of the original right of punition almost to the total exclusion of a thorough consideration of punishment, and the various punishments themselves. All this is very well in its place; so we may say many spirited and perhaps sound things on the culinary disposition of man in the abstract; why man cooks, and how he distinguishes himself by cookery from the brute creation; but when we finally come to the dinner itself, we have to talk about the various nourishments after all.

10. Finally, I may say a few words on those theories, which derive the right of punition from the principle of self-defence, vested in its fullest amplitude in each individual when that so called state of nature existed, which is believed to have preceded the state. It is supposed that the latter once being founded, self-defence passes over from the individual to the state, or its chief magistrate. It is unnecessary here to say anything about the fabled state of nature, which, in fact, would be a very unnatural one. All we have to observe in the present place is, that this theory alone would lead us to nothing else but the merest expediency. For self-defence, or self-preservation places every means at our disposal, in the choice of which we are guided, if in that presumed state of nature, by our own will and views—in short, by expediency alone.

To give a sketch, a very brief and hasty one indeed, of my views on this subject, I shall speak of the following points, in the succession in which they appear here:

What is punishment?

On what ground rests the punitory power, or whence do we derive penal right?

What is the standard of punishment?

What is the object of punishment? which leads us to consider:

What characteristic traits ought punishment to possess, and what ought to be excluded from it, according to the compound demand of justice, the object of punishment and the psychologic state of the offence to be punished?

Does solitary confinement at labor answer the demands thus established, and are the objections made against this punitory system, or some of them, substantial, well-founded and candid?

The state is a society founded on right, or it is human society in as far as it constitutes itself and acts upon the principle of right.* Right is taken here in its primordial sense, as that

* For those who by profession or taste have made the state a subject of especial reflection, I may be allowed to mention by way of note, what, in a popular essay, would have found no befitting place in the text. The word right being constantly used in the English language to denote some specific right, a privilege or title, does not convey in the above connexion so distinct and definite a notion, as a philosophic treatment of the subject demands. Perspicuity respecting elementary notions is all-important. We want a word which, with reference to state, corresponds to the word religious with reference to church. We say a church is a religious society, united by a common bond of discipline, e. g. the Gallican church, Presbyterian church. It would be evidently turning in a circle, were we to say a church (ecclesia) is an ecclesiastical society. It would amount to the same as if we were to assert that a lion is a leonine animal. To say, therefore, the state (πολις) is a political society, says nothing; for *political* is nothing more than the adjective corresponding to the substantive noun *state*, which deceives us, being derived from a different idiom. Had the English language adopted the Greek noun *polis*, as well as the adjective, the circle would appear at once. This want was severely felt in writing the work already mentioned; yet it was absolutely necessary clearly to express the idea. I have, therefore, not hesitated to form the word *jural* from the Latin *jus*, analogous to *rural* from *rus*. Unnecessarily coining new words is an evidence of weakness, want of knowledge or taste; to hesitate promptly to form a word when the true want exists, is a slavish submission of the mind to the language, the object to the means. By the adoption of this word all difficulty vanishes. The state is essentially a jural society, and all relations in it, or in other words,

which gives the foundation of all single rights. It is the regulation and fixation of the use of individual moral freedom, which each man possesses as man, as rational and moral beings placed in society, that is co-ordinately with others; it originates out of the just demand each one makes to enjoy this freedom. All that the state, therefore, demands or gives, or all that the individual demands at its hands and yields to it; in short, all relations of the individual to the state, must be founded on right, or the idea of the just.

The difficulty of finding a firm basis for civil punition, and the great variety of opinions respecting this subject have arisen from this very fact. We cannot do, or ought not to do anything within the sphere of the state, for which we do not first establish the right we may have to do it. In domestic punition the same difficulty does not exist. No one can doubt the *natural* relation between child and parent. The child is naturally dependent upon its parents, physically, morally and intellectually; or, in other words, for support and education. The object of domestic punishment is improvement. It arises out of the natural relation of the family. In the state, however, we have first to prove a right, we may have to improve morally or intellectually, in certain given circumstances, or cases; for it is by no means the direct object of the state to educate or morally to improve every member of it. The general object of the state is, as I have said, the protection of that freedom which each individual has a right to claim as a moral being. Another difficulty has arisen out of an opposite error.

It is, moreover, a grave mistake of nearly all who have given a theory of the state and its attributes, that as soon as they had construed, as they imagined, the state, they left society entirely out of view, as if merged in, absorbed by the state. Yet society continues to exist with distinct attributes, even after

---

all political relations are of a jural character; if not, they do not strictly belong to the state. I doubt whether any better word can be proposed, the Greek language has no distinct word expressing the sense of the Latin *jus* in this meaning, namely *quid sit justum*—that which is rightful. I shall, however, always be found ready to adopt any better word, if offered.

all those which are founded on the idea of right, are concentrated in and form the state; and not only does society continue to exist, as such, but the closest connexion between the two must forever remain. We find an instance in public opinion, which is an attribute of society; when it passes over into the state and becomes public will. The state is the ægis of society, and it has likewise to redress toward individuals wrongs, which society may have committed or produced by its peculiar organization. This connexion between the two is every where important, and not the least so in matters of punishment, as we shall see hereafter. Many jurists, I repeat, have fallen into errors, in treating of punishments, because they kept in view the state alone, and either forgot or did not suspect the connexion of state and society, which is no fusion, but a connexion of two distinct things. Yet the state is nothing artificial, nothing made, that may or may not be adopted. It is necessary, and therefore natural, grown, and indispensable. It is a necessary manifestation of society. If we now call right, that which indicates man's relation to the state, or that which is the necessary consequence of his relations founded on the just, toward others, that which the state is bound to grant him, punishment is the right between society and the offender, or, however paradoxical it may appear at first glance, the right both of the society and the offender. But why is it so? Merely because it is necessary, and farther we cannot go? By no means. In order to prove that punishment be what we have asserted it to be, we have to show first that it be just, secondly that it be necessary. All idea of the just is essentially founded upon equality; without it, as its first foundation, justice cannot be imagined. Every individual in the state must grant to others the right he claims for himself: if he interferes with the rightful state of others, he grants them the abstract right to interfere with his.

The lex talionis starts undoubtedly from the right point, from perfect evenness, but it stops short of a most important item, without which we act wrong in inflicting injury. The abstract principle of injury for injury, which is the principle of the lex talionis, pervades the whole sphere of human actions, from those between individuals, expressed in the homely alliteration "tit for tat," to the highest international actions. He who injures me gives me an abstract right to inflict injury on him. He who beats me gives the abstract right of beating him. I speak here, as I am bound to do, of the abstract right, that is, of that which is founded on strict justice and on nothing else, not of actions which may be prompted by generosity, charity or prudence. Now the principle of the law of retaliation, sufferance for sufferance, which exists between individuals, passes over into the state, for the state is a society in which every one individually owes certain duties to every one collectively. The principle of perfect evenness is retained, for man must, by his nature, live in society, otherwise he cannot live fully as man; that is, he cannot become that for which his maker has placed him on this earth. Society, again, cannot exist without the ægis of the state. It is, therefore, not at the option of the individual to consider himself insulated and independent, or as a member of the state. He is by his nature a member of the state, and the state, on the other hand, has a natural right to pay injury with injury, because each interference with the rights of the individual, is an interference with itself, or a wrong inflicted upon itself, as soon as the rightful state of things has been disturbed.

We have to mention two more points: first, the state being a society of moral beings, because right can only exist between these, each *public* immorality becomes as such an interference with the rights of the citizens, and gives the state a right to produce injury for the injury done, though prudence may dictate not to make use of the right. Secondly, every dangerous act, if knowingly done, becomes a wrong, an immoral act, interferes with the rights of the citizens, who demand protection from the state. If a man lets loose a tiger among men, it is certainly an immoral act, though he need not have absolutely intended to cause thereby the death of others. To injure a dyke in Holland is highly immoral, because highly dangerous to the lives and property of the community. To light a fire on the sea-shore is in itself an innocent act, but the danger for the mariners, who may mistake it for a light-house, makes it justly a highly penal act.

The important point, in which the law of retaliation lacked, is this:

Punishment implies the idea of an application or infliction of some evil or sufferance. In doing anything, however, which involves a sufferance for another, it is not sufficient that we have the abstract right of doing it, but we must have a good object in view, in making use of this right, else it becomes useless infliction of suffering—in other words, cruelty. The state stands with regard to the offender precisely on the same footing as to its right of punishing, as the parent stands respecting his child. The father or mother have a right to punish the child, but if no good object is kept in view in making use of this abstract right, the act becomes cruelty. The Roman law already acknowledges that no one shall make use of his abstract right merely to the disadvantage of another, and without use or interest to himself. What would we think of an individual who would inflict injury, solely because injury had been done to him, for no use or benefit whatever to him, the injurer, or any one else? We would say that he is actuated by vengeance. How much more blameable, then, would be the state which, according to its true essence, is without vindictiveness or passion, if it were to inflict sufferance simply because it has the abstract right to inflict it! The law of retaliation, taken in its material character alone—eye for eye—would be in many cases uselessly harsh, in others it might mislead to a very erroneous leniency, or almost total absence of punishment; for instance, should a thief who has stolen a small sum, be punished merely by giving up the stolen sum, and paying over and above an equivalent to the robbed individual?

We arrive, then, at this important point: that though equality and the idea on which the state is founded, give us the abstract right of retaliation, we can make use of it only so far as it shall be found necessary. And how far is it necessary?

Before I answer this point I beg leave to make another remark.

Man, as has been said already, is a moral being, i. e. a being endowed with a moral character. Wherever he goes, whatever institution he forms, he carries this attribute with him. Without it no relations of right, no rights themselves can exist between men. There are no rights between animals. He must, therefore, maintain this first of all attributes inviolate; and every committed wrong is not only the material wrong done to our neighbor, but the moral wrong of interference with the rights of others. A society in which every sort of wrong might be committed with impunity, would necessarily lose its ethical character, and a community loses in its ethical character in the same degree as wrongs remain unpunished. The expression of public disapproval of wrong would be missing. The greatest injury suffered by a community, in which murders are frequently committed with impunity, is by no means the insecurity of life. After counting all the lives lost by bloody rencontres, it might be found that the number is far below the deaths occasioned in another community by imprudent exposure to a changeable climate. Would this justify the former community in continuing to leave murders unpunished? It is the lowering of the moral standard, a necessary consequence of trifling with the highest object in creation—with man himself, which forms the most baneful consequence of such a state of things. The state, therefore, has to punish all offences against its laws—for according to its nature, it has no cognizance over others, no organ, as it were, to perceive them —likewise as offences against its necessary character, and must not become unjust by arbitrarily punishing some, and at other times omit punishment of the same offences. I wish not to be misunderstood as if I meant to assert that immorality alone can constitute the punishableness of an action to be visited by political authority. On the contrary, immorality without any other concomitant, would form no ground for making use of the right of punishment which we have acquired as indicated already; because the science of politics proves that nothing is more dangerous than the intermeddling of the state with private affairs; secondly, that no punishment can in justice take place, where no violation of right has taken place. This is now generally adopted by all the most profound jurists, and is, in fact, to be deduced from the principle of the right of punishment, which I have just laid down, namely, reciprocity on the ground of equality. I shall speak, however, once of the fact already alluded to, that immorality may become the ground of punishableness *when* and *because* it interferes with the rights of others.

It is on this ground, likewise, that the state has a right to punish shameful and offensive cruelty against animals, as, from sheer malignance, to the dishonor of man is sometimes practised. The animal, indeed, has no right, and therefore no legal offence against it can be committed: but if the cruelty is committed publicly, it is an offence against the rights of citizens who see it, for they have a right to claim that no such revolting acts be committed in their presence. The fact that the animal is the property of its tormentor does not excuse, for no citizen has the right to do with his property absolutely what he chooses. There are many acts which I am not permitted to do, though they affect directly my own property only. The danger is another ground on which we have the right and the duty to punish barbarity against animals, for, as has been stated, to do what is dangerous is immoral, and members of the state who can in cold blood torture an animal for the sake of torturing it, are surely most dangerous to society.

Thirdly, immorality alone does not afford a ground of punishment, because the state would not reach it by its punishments. Immorality as such, is to be reached by society, not by the state; by public opinion, the many relations of respectability in the community, &c., and is to be prevented by good, sound and general education, and if it has already acquired a character of danger with the young, by those excellent and benevolent establishments called houses of refuge, *into* which we acquire a *right* of placing the young offender, by the *danger* he offers to society, and *in* which we do not punish, but endeavor to correct and rescue, on account of the youth of the offender, which does not make him yet strictly accountable to the state, whose active member he has not yet become. The youthful offender, moreover, has a right to demand correction at the hands of society, because his youth is of itself a proof that he has become corrupt, in a great degree, by circumstances, that is, by unfortunate, yet perhaps unavoidable relations of society itself. What is the standard of punishment? This question is closely connected with the next: what is the object of punishment?

The first object of the state is the protection of its members —the citizens, or security. Security means that state in which the citizen is protected against any violation of his rights, and by which the great and general object of the state is secured. The object of the state, however, is the fully obtaining the ends of man as man. He cannot obtain them except in society; man is absolutely made for society; and this society has to secure itself, and to remove all obstacles in the way of obtaining its ends, which forms the object of the state. Now this security is of twofold character: material and intellectual, direct or indirect. Direct security I call the positive protection against direct wrong, i. e. interference with the individual rights of others. Indirect security I call that security which results from the maintenance of that general state of society, without which its ends cannot be obtained. Every immoral act, therefore, declared to be such by the state, is an act against this security, for without the moral state of society it cannot exist; it is, consequently, an interference with the rights of all its members. But this does not yet give us the privilege of making use of the general right of punishment thus acquired, because there may be other powers far more effective, to repress it, as we have seen already, or the punishments possibly at the disposal of the state may not reach the evil, and thus punishment would be useless, i. e. cruel, or the danger of interfering with it may be greater than the advantage to be derived from its punishment; or finally, the wrong may not be sufficiently definable for the state, in order to bring it clearly under a category of punishable acts. Circumstances, moreover, necessarily connected with punishment, especially publicity of trial, may render the punishment a far greater evil to the security of the state, than the punishable act itself. It is thus, for instance, the case, according to the opinion of many, and for one, of myself, respecting certain vile offences, too vile to be named, which public opinion justly visits with far severer punishment than any human code could fix on them, and which on that account are committed in darkness and privacy; while the trial drags them into light and injures thus far more. Nay, several of these vile and disgusting acts are, as long as secretly committed, no violation of others—of human beings, which they could become only by being publicly done. If, however, at any time, a part of society should sink so low that these unnatural vices should become general, society would have a right and, it may be, a duty in punishing them.

The true standard of punishment, therefore, that is, the standard of the degree how far we are justified in making use of the previously acquired general right of punishment, is:

1. Danger—material or intellectual danger to society.

2. The effect the punishment has on society, or the punished individual himself. If it has no effect on either, it is useless; though the desired effect is by no means merely the momentary one of deterring from crime, but also the general and far more important one of keeping up public feeling of right, that is, a public feeling that the state is a society of right, and cannot allow the violation of rights unpunished. If the punishment has any effect on the individual, we are likewise justified in applying it on the ground of security; we protect by punishing. To reform the inward man of the offender would, of itself, afford no right to punish, because that is his affair; but by his offence he has shown that his moral condition is of a kind that it becomes dangerous to society; we have, therefore, not only a right, but also the obligation to reform him, provided the state have means at its disposal to obtain this desirable end.

If, therefore, an interference with the rights of others has taken place, the danger of society affords the standard of punishment. Frequently the danger itself is, in turn, the sole standard of the interference with the rights of others, as I have mentioned already. A great historian* informs us, that it was a capital offence in the village of Ursern, in Switzerland, to cut a single tree of an ancient grove, high above it, because these trees alone protected the inhabitants from avalanches. Was it wrong in those people to affix the highest punishment to this act? Surely as little as the high penalties with which treason is visited, because it is an interference with the primary rights of the people—security in enjoying life.

Two reasons demand, moreover, that the punishment be just, i. e. that offence and punishment stand, according to the moral views of the people, in proper relation. In fact, the principle of retaliation necessarily involves this; for if the punishment be, according to the views of the society, too hard, it means nothing less than that retaliation has been exceeded. The two additional reasons are these: 1. The state is founded upon the idea of the just; destroy justice, and you destroy the essence of the state. Disproportionate punishments, however—whether disproportionately heavy or light, are unjust. 2. The effect of the punishment is destroyed. If too light, the offender as well as the community feel that there is no justice in the punishment, and the moral belief in the state, or public feeling of justice will be weakened or destroyed. If too severe, it will have the same effect with the addition that it alienates the offender still more from society, an effect which is, as we shall see hereafter, most diligently to be avoided, not by way of charity, but on strict grounds of justice on the part of the state. The necessity of punishment, before we acquire a full right actually to punish, leads us a step farther, and we find that not every illegal act is punishable; for instance, in those cases in which a restitution of the injury done, or a public declaration that no offence against the character of the injured person had been meant by the offensive words of the injurer, are entirely sufficient. Punishment in this case would

* Johannes Müller, Swiss History, 2d Book, chap. I, note 159.

go beyond what is necessary, and therefore unjust. Punishment takes place when the avowal of wrong is not sufficient, when the protection of the rights of the offended demand it, or when rights have been violated which can never be re-established, (e. g. in case of murder,) and the rights of others demand protection. Disproportion between offence and punishment is at once acknowledged as unjust. If the papers of the time have reported correctly, a lad, named James Death, aged fifteen years, was sentenced to death, in the year 1837, in England, by Mr. Justice Tolman, for having robbed on the king's highway another lad, of buns, pork-pies, &c., with threats to kill the latter, if he would not give up the edibles. The fact that no reader believes in the possibility of this sentence having been executed, shows the injustice of the law.

I cannot pass over to the next point without once more referring to the meaning in which I have used the word effect. I do not mean the momentary and always accidental effect, but the general, or the belief of the community in the state, namely, that it is a society which rests on the idea of the just, which cannot exist without ethical ground. If wrong, however, does not meet with evil consequences, the moral character of the state is thereby alone destroyed. To take the momentary and accidental effect, as the principle of gradation of punishment, leads to the theory of deterring, which is, probably, the very worst of all false penal theories; to tearing and pinching with red hot tongs, cutting the tongue, and putting out the eyes; and lends the cloak of principle to unprincipled revenge.

As the effect of punishment is a necessary element of its gradation, it is clear that the latter must, in a great measure, depend:

1. Upon the material and intellectual state of society.
2. Upon the view society takes of the offence.
3. Upon the view society takes of the punishment.
4. Upon the general psychologic state of the class of offenders.
5. Upon the operation of punishment in any other respect.

I have read, I believe in the Memoirs of Prince de Ligne,

that Catharine II. related that Peter the Great—if I am not much mistaken—changed some severe sentence against several noblemen, into this: that they should receive a box on the ear, in the public market, by the hangman: and, added the empress, it was a wise and great principle which guided him; he wanted to impart the feeling of honor to his nobility, the offence having been a highly dishonorable act.

It will be seen that, the original right of punishment once settled, all the various objects, such as protection, warning, reform, expediency, from which it was believed possible to derive the first punitory right of the state, come in as *motives* of punishment, or in other words, as reasons why we make use of the right of punishment already existing.

From the principles which have been ascertained, as from others laid down by the theory of penal law, or relating to human actions in general, we find that sound punishment must possess, among others, the following characteristics:

1. Inasmuch as punishment is a human action by which certain objects are to be obtained, the common rules of action are applicable to it:

We must strive to produce the greatest effect with the fewest means.

The means we use must effect the object we wish to obtain.

They must not defeat or counteract the object we strive for.

Still less must the means increase or generate the evil which we labor to counteract.

Finally, in order to obtain a general result we must act on a general plan, according to fixed principles.

2. All punishment must be founded in the right we have to punish, derived from the essential character of the state, as that society which rests on the idea of the just.

3. This right can be actually made use of only so far as is necessary and useful. Without this it is useless—cruel.

4. The great and final object of punishment is protection in its highest adaptation.

5. The principle of gradation of punishment is the danger of society, yet it must remain within the bounds of justice.

6. That punishment must have the effect it is intended to have, is another reason why it must be just; and a principle which guides in the adaptation of the punishment to the offence. It must be just, therefore, according to the spirit of the age.

7. Punishment, in order to be just, must proceed from the state, and neither be left to private revenge, nor to the private view of the judge. Those, therefore, err greatly, who with Sir Thomas More, in his Utopia, demand that the penal judges should have their hands entirely free, and assign punishment according to the combination of all the given circumstances, only guided by their virtue and conscience. Modern penal codes have been called by some, who dream of the perfection of patriarchic governments, penal price currents. No person, acquainted with the subject, has ever insisted upon an absolute fixation of punishments. Bodin was opposed to tariffs of punishments. The ancients acted on the principle adopted by Sir T. More. Lycurgus left it to the judges alone to settle the punishment; nor was the Areopagus bound by any law in assigning punishment; but we must not forget that penal law was then in its incipient stage, and that, according to the views of the ancients, the individual was all that it was, in and through the state alone, absorbed by it, while with us the individual is the object of the state. Protection, our great end of the state, requires fixed penal codes.

8. It is useless to talk against punishment as men like Coleridge have done, (see his Letters and Conversations,) and lately Thomas Walker, Esq., one of the police magistrates of the metropolis, (London,) because it will never abolish crime. They show that they have never thoroughly understood what punishment essentially is. If they assert that by education, removal of pauperism, &c., crime will be abolished, they forget that the human heart will always remain a focus of passion, and that the more civilized a nation is, the more intricate are its relations, which will always induce some to commit offences, and that with increased variety of human activity, increased opportunity of crime takes place. No physician ever pretended that medicine would eradicate disease among men.

9. That if the punishment be just, it must be capable of graduation, and the more capable of graduation the better.

10. Yet that it be just and considered as such, it ought to be as even and uniform as possible. Uniformity and graduableness, are two of the greatest desiderata in punishments.

11. The state knows of no revenge; by revenge it would lower itself to the offender. The state in punishing, protects, and not only the community at large, but it continues to protect the offender as long as he remains within it, i. e. as long as he lives.

12. Punishment is not intended to atone; to wipe off and nullify the offence. This cannot be done, except by a repenting heart before a benignant deity, with regard to the immorality of the offence alone, and has consequently nothing to do with the state. What has been done is done, and cannot be undone as fact. "One thing," says Agathon in Aristotle, Ethics 6, ch. 3, "One thing even the gods cannot do, to undo that which is done."

13. Punishment ought to be calm in its character; it ought calmly to operate, and keep the true mean between trifling leniency and harsh cruelty. Cruelty is weakness. Strong governments, i. e. governments which have grown out of and provide faithfully for the true wants of the people, can afford to be mild. A mild punishment strikes deeper than a cruel one, for it carries the whole weight of public opinion and that of the offender himself along with it.

14. The state, being the agent of society, in punishing, and having the obligation of protecting even the offender, has the duty of aiding as far as able, the possible reform of the offender, because society does not know by what fault of her own, e. g. bad laws, neglect in general education, the offender has become such.

15. The state has the most solemn duty,

a. Not to make the offender worse than he was, when he came within its penal action.

b. To remove everything that probably will, or possibly may make the offender worse.

16. The state has the right of turning the punishment of the individual to the greatest legitimate advantage of society, provided punishment is founded on a previous indisputable right, and meted out according to justice, and not according to advantage. The state, therefore, acquires the right to use the punishment as example, as prevention of crime with the offender himself, &c.

17. The state, which has no right to interfere with the moral state of any loyal citizen, acquires it with regard to the offender, who, by committing offence, has fallen within its sphere of penal action; for it is one of the means of prevention of crime, which the protection of society requires. By the offence the offender has shown that he is in a moral state dangerous to society.

18. The offender, who has not committed his offence from sudden passion, or prompted by powerful circumstances, as great misery of a parent, &c., considers himself at war with society, out of its pale; he sees no reciprocal relation and obligation between the two. It is thus cause and effect of many crimes. The state has few surer means of re-establishing this feeling of loyalty, without which an offenceless state of the individual is not imaginable, than by teaching him to work. It protects society and him by doing so. Labor, and learning to work, calms the mind and furnishes one of the requisites of an honest life.

19. The state, in endeavoring to reunite the offender with society, has carefully to obviate renewed irritation, which cannot but prevent the feeling of loyalty. If the punishment irritates, provokes, exasperates, it defeats its own object.

20. Far the greater part of crimes are committed from original thoughtlessness. Crime is prevented, by making the criminal thoughtful.

21. If it be desirable that the offender should feel reunited to society, the state must avoid what would hinder this, for instance, acquaintance even by sight, with other offenders.

22. Punishment as to what it is to consist of, is to be regulated

a. By the state of society.

b. By the psychologic state of the offender.

c. By experience, including national character.

d. By our knowledge of man in general.

e. By the means at our disposal.

23. The state must not challenge by trifling punishments. Punishment must make a lasting impression. Nor must it defeat its own moral effect by disproportionate severity, still less by cruelty.

24. Certainty of punishment is more important than the degree of sufferance produced by it, because it flows from, and, in turn, maintains and diffuses a sense of justice, of the ethic character and importance of man, and a belief in the morality of the state. Respecting the transgressor, the fact that punishment will undoubtedly follow, impresses the evil-disposed far more effectually than that the punishment will be severe, provided it does follow. Every man calculates chances in his favor, even the soldier scaling the breach.

25. If punishment ought to be certain, both in its being actually the consequence of transgression, and in its degree, it ought on the other hand strike the offender alone, as much as this is possible in human society, in which all members are so closely interlinked. Hence exceptions are justly made of pregnant or nursing women, respecting some punishments.

26. Punishment ought to be in its nature, as calculable as possible; that is, it ought to be so, that those who inflict it should be able to calculate its effects, or remain master over it as much as possible. Defamatory punishments, therefore, are bad, because they affect different individuals differently. Hence, likewise, should punishment depend as little as possible upon the prison keepers. They should not have it in their power much to aggravate or alleviate.

27. Punishment ought to be accommodable in its nature. By accommodable punishment I mean that which accommodates itself, by its own nature, to the given case. If an absolute fine be imposed for an offence, it is not accommodable, because the rich do not feel it, and it is heavy for the poor. If putting in irons and working on the high road be imposed, it

is a far severer punishment to the well-educated, than to an uneducated offender, who had few ties with society, and yet the better education itself, may have been one of the aiding causes of the offence; for instance, in order to support a family in a decent manner. So the punishment ought to accommodate itself to sex, age, habit of reflection, keenness of honor, &c.

28. Punishment must be a sufferance of some sort, whether by way of privation or infliction; else it is no punishment. We shall see that privation is far preferable.

29. Only accountable beings, i. e. persons physically and intellectually free in their volition, are punishable. Insane persons, children, people in their second childhood, sleep-walkers, people who act by surprise, or under duresse, are either not at all accountable, or not so with regard to certain actions.

It is, therefore, degrading the woman, if a sickly feeling of vague honor or philanthropy prevents us from punishing female offenders, for we deny them, thereby, the degree of accountability they have an undoubted right to demand. First, woman was considered the slave of the parents or husband, or at least too much subjected to them to have any high degree of accountability of herself. The christian religion aided powerfully in raising the rights of woman, as can be shown by history. King Magnus Erichson of Sweden decreed in 1335: "the woman must atone for all her crimes, like the man."* And now we begin again to deny them their accountability and to treat them like children, or as if they were too weak to be fully accountable, or as if they offered but little danger; while it requires no uncommon knowledge of criminal matters to be aware of the fact, that a woman once sunk to crime, and even only to vice, is one of the most dangerous members of the community.† The reasons why it should be so, can be very clearly traced, though the limits of the present lines do

* Geijer, History of Sweden, in Heeren and Uckert, vol. I. p. 273.

† See my *Introduction* to de Beaumont and de Tocqueville *on the Penitentiary System in America.*

not permit me to do so. Napoleon's opinion on this subject, as given in O'Meara, coincides with this.

29. Correction can never afford us a principle for the duration of punishment; because reform is something on which we cannot insist, nor can we measure it with any distinctness, sufficient to ground acts of justice upon it. If we cannot insist on it, we become unjust toward those who do not reform, and are obliged to suffer longer.

30. Punishment ought to be founded, first of all on a physical basis, because this alone affords a sure and safe basis; and evenness of punishment can take place only when we have gained that basis. The moral state of the individual is not directly tangible by the state. But the punishment ought to be so that it does not prevent moral effects, or positively produces bad ones. It is desirable that punishment, though founded upon a physical basis, as incarceration, do not consist in physical pain, because pain irritates.

31. Punishment presupposes an individual to be punished, within the sphere of the state, and who is accountable. The dead or the unborn are not accountable, because they cannot account. Hence all so called punishments, which are directed against the dead, e. g. disinterment and placing the body on the gallows, or degradation of future generations, are inadmissible.

32. The state, in punishing, must never sink to the level of the offender; hence punishments increased by cruelty are inadmissible, for they originate from wrath and hatred, not from justice.

33. Avoid even all appearance that you punish, because the offender has *dared* to disobey; that is, as if you punished chiefly because your authority has been offended, not because the authority is for the common good, and *therefore* defying it, is an offence—is immoral. The very expression offending the authority, is making it personal; a person, a moral individual, may be offended, the state as such—its authorities cannot. They may be defied, disobeyed, but cannot be offended. Incalcula-

ble evil has flowed from this unhappy confusion of the ideas of personality and political authority.

34. It is impossible for the state to ascertain with any degree of certainty to act upon, the psychologic state of the offender, and the entire relation between his whole inward man and the offence he has committed. God alone is that supreme and absolute judge, who can do it, and who will truly deal out to every one according to his deeds. We mortal men cannot even frequently find out, whether an offence seems to warrant in us a belief that it will be but the forerunner of many, according to the depraved state of the offender, or whether it was the sudden or peculiar action, provoked by a peculiar combination of circumstances. Yet the character of the offence, depends greatly upon the individual within. How then shall we act? We have to ascertain a sort of punishment, which will adapt, accommodate itself even to this circumstance, as much as possible.

35. The offence must be punished; yet the offender alone should be punished. Who is the offender, the person that did the deed, or they who brought him up with all possible examples of vice and crime, as the children of offenders often are? Punishment, therefore, ought to enter as much as possible into the individuality of the trespasser. It ought to possess this quality in its nature.

36. He who has the right to dispose temporarily, or for life, of my personal liberty, has the undoubted right to dispose of my labor; for it is but a continuation and consequence of the limitation of my volition, in which the essential character of imprisonment or privation of liberty consists.

37. Punition, considered with regard to the future actions of the offender, aims at political reform or outward loyalty. Let us remove, therefore, every thing from it, which interferes with this subject, and connect with it every thing which promotes it, and which we have a right to connect with the punishment.

38. That punishment be certain, both in its being applied to each necessary case, and its effect on society. let it be so that

those who have to apply it, do it willingly, actively, and promptly, and those who are to benefit by it, concur readily in its justice. (See 5.)

39. The state, in applying a punishment, which by its nature operates upon, or appeals to the more essentially human qualities in the offender, has it in its power to raise him, in his own estimation, and, indirectly, to raise the whole criminal community.

The truth and justice of these remarks are either evident at first glance, or will be found so by a degree of reflection which does not stand in need of any aid by special experience in these matters. At least, I believe that I may safely make this observation with regard to nearly all of them; and respecting the others, they are so well ascertained by all persons conversant with penologic matters, that I fear contradiction on no side. Those who have never paid any attention to this subject of vital importance, may, for instance, not know that far the greatest majority of offenders consider or feel themselves at war with the community, either for real or supposed wrongs received at their hands, or for some other perverse train of reasoning; for the criminal logic, as it well might be termed, is very curious, and, frequently, not without consistency, if we once grant some terms. Yet every one who knows convicts will agree with me on this point, and, probably, likewise, that it is the very one which must be defeated, before any political or moral reform can become possible. It is at the same time the most difficult point in penology, because it requires an acknowledgment not only of the justice of the punishment, (according to the established laws) but likewise of its justness (according to the fundamental principles of human variety)—it requires, in short, humiliation before power—power that has shown itself successful, victorious; which is one of the most difficult acts in every human breast, not originally from depravity, but from that noble disposition in every man to resist mere force and violence. Every convict lives but over, in his limited sphere, the racking ambition of Milton's Satan. If you once gain so much over the convict as to make him calm, and to feel no spirit of resistance or defiance against the prison, whatever he may yet feel as to the judge, his sentence, and society at large, you have made the first step toward that great desirable end. But to obtain this you must not irritate him anew; you must awaken in him the conviction that apart from the sentence and your strict execution of it, you are in nowise his enemy, his tormenter, and likewise that the sentence is firm and unalterable. Otherwise his whole intellectual energy and activity are directed to this point, that, perhaps by pardon, by influence of others, &c., his punishment may be shortened. For the same reason does the hope held out that good behavior will abbreviate punishment, operate badly. The internal process toward possible reform is quite a different one, and far sterner. The convict cannot be reformed except he considers the sentence and consequent punishment as a *fact*, no longer to be altered, as his *lot*. He has first to acknowledge his punishment as unavoidable, then as necessary in principle, and finally as his friend. I do not speak here of philanthropic dreams; I speak from facts and personal observations, corroborated by prisoners themselves and their guardians, as I like to call their guards. In France a law was passed, some years ago, which held out the hope of shorter imprisonment as a reward for good behavior, and the effect was so bad that it was abolished. Mr. de la Ville de Mirmont says that he caused the law dated February 6, 1818, to be passed, and that frequently he had repented of it.*

Let us represent to our mind the pith of the above remarks, and then examine the various punishments accordingly.

Punishment, with regard to its principle, ought to be:

I. A sufferance, (28.)

II. Just, (5, 6, 7, 9, 10, 13, &c.)

III. Striking the offender alone, (25.)

* Page 55 of his Observations on Central Houses of Detention, &c., Paris 1833. Mr. de Mirmont was inspector-general of the Central Prisons, a gentleman of practical knowledge, therefore.

With regard to its effect:

IV. It ought to prevent crime:

By warning the community, (16.)

By correcting the offender, politically or morally, (37.)

By maintaining the moral character of the state.

V. It ought to protect.

With regard to its administration:

VI. It ought to be certain, (24.)

VII. Free from revenge, cruelty, (32, 33.)

VIII. Calm, (13.)

With regard to its qualities:

IX. It ought to be graduable, (9.)

X. " " accommodable, (27.)

XI. " " calculable, (26.)

XII. " " uniform, (10.)

With regard to its psychologic effect on the offender:

XIII. It ought not to irritate, (19.)

XIV. " to make thoughtful, (20.)

XV. " not to provoke, (23.)

XVI. " to adapt itself to the individuality of the offender, (34, 35.)

With regard to the state:

XVII. The state has the most sacred duty not to make the convict worse, (15.)

XVIII. It has a right to reform, (17.)

XIX. It has a duty to do so, (14.)

XX. It should endeavor to reunite the offender to society, (18, 36.)

XXI. It has a right and a duty to make the convict work, (18, 36.)

XXII. It must annihilate all causes of crime, wherever it has a right to act, (within or without the convict.)

Of all the punishments now more or less in use we shall examine the following:

Apology.

Publicly asking pardon.

Fine.

Ridicule.
Censure.
Dishonor.
Declaration of unworthiness of public confidence.
Privation of privileges.
Degradation.
Distinction in dress.
Infamation of the offender.
" of his descendants.
Pillory.
Whipping.
Public whipping.
Branding.
Infliction of pain otherwise than by whipping.
Imprisonment.
Imprisonment with public labor.
Exile.
Transportation.
Maiming.
Death.
Death with additional pains or infamatory procedures.

Apology.—(*Amende honorable,*) asking pardon publicly. Strictly speaking, we cannot count the asking pardon publicly a punishment within the sphere of the state; for obliging an individual to ask for something which it is not in the power of the state to oblige another to grant, is futile. The state cannot force me to pardon, because it is a strictly moral act, over which the state has no control. If, however, we substitute for it a public declaration of honor, an avowal that no offence was meant by certain words, and that the offender has no intention of injuring the reputation of the offended, or that, though he meant an offence, he is now sorry for having used certain words, it is in certain cases a wise punishment. Being sorry for what we have done is a strictly moral act indeed, but the state has power over the declaration of this sentiment, if the law allows it as an alternative, either to make this declaration, or to undergo a real punishment. The *amende honor-*

able is important where honor is considered by the law as a civil right, and it ought to be considered so everywhere. With us the feeling of honor exists in a high degree in society, yet the state does not acknowledge it as such, but only inasmuch as reputation is connected with the external welfare of the individual. The consequence is, that the offended individual seeks redress in another way—by the duel. I do not pretend to say that duels would cease by the introduction of the *amende* into our codes, but it would lead to a rarer occurrence of them; at any rate, it would be doing justice to society, in which the feeling of honor does exist, and which, according to our social relations, ought to be protected as such. Why it has not been received as a civil right, which must be therefore protected by the state, into our legislation, can be easily shown from the history of English law, but it is no reason that it ought not to be received. The general principle of human actions, that we ought always to endeavor to obtain the greatest possible effect by the smallest means, applies to this subject. Why resort to stricter punishments, fine, &c., if we can, in most cases, obtain the object by fair and much milder means?

Fine.—All nations, which acknowledge the value of private property, have adopted fine as a punishment, and justly so; but it ought to be applied with caution. Fine ought never to be allowed to be imposed for offences of a graver kind, because the punishment would bear too much the character of buying off guilt; necessarily high, would establish an unjust, invidious and mischievous distinction between the poor and the rich. We call fine, of course, only that exaction of money which is imposed over and above the restitution for some injury done.

Ridicule.—If used with great caution and so that it does not embitter, ridicule may be advantageously used in military punition, in fact everywhere where the individuals form a close community, and where discipline is to be maintained. I have seen good effects of it in the army. It is not, however, to be used in civil punition, for it would assume at once the character of public dishonor. Besides, the offences for which the state punishes, are necessarily of too grave a kind, demanding more than ridicule.

Censure.—This punishment, which we only know in legislative assemblies, or, in some states for offences of civil or military officers, ought, I have no doubt in my mind, to be introduced in civil punition likewise. I doubt not but that it will be introduced with the advancement of civilization. It would be in many cases sufficient, though mild. It is surprising that it has not been adopted in some of the many new penal codes, drawn up within the last fifteen years, many of which have so excellent features and have been compiled with the utmost patience and great knowledge. We have done one thing with the advance of civilization, namely, abolished unfit punishments; we must do more, adopt new punishments, demanded by the changed state of society.

Dishonor.—Publicly declaring an offender as dishonored is a bad punishment. It affects the hardened little, the sensitive too much, and injures all *beyond* the proper limits of punishment, because it destroys the relations of the offender to society for ever; it cuts him off, instead of bringing him back to it. The punishment is not *accommodable* nor *calculable;* in fact, the state has no right to dishonor, to offend the inner man. If dishonor is the natural consequence of other rightful acts, it is different. I here speak only of dishonor as such.

Declaration of unworthiness of public confidence, Privation of privileges; Degradation.—The first has been adopted among others by the new Norwegian code; the second and third are in use among most civilized nations. It is a rightful punishment if it be nothing more than the public declaration of the natural consequence of penal acts. If a citizen have rendered himself unworthy of public confidence, the state has the right, and in many cases the duty, to declare his unfitness for those places for which it is requisite. If a citizen have shown by crimes that he is unfit to exercise the privileges of a citizen, be it the common privileges or some peculiar one, the state is bound to declare it, else it neglects the general protection and allows the privileges, the more important the more they come down to practical life, to sink into disregard—one of the greatest afflictions of a free country. To vote, and to sit as juror, are most sacred rights. Degradation, where grades exist, as in the army, is likewise a perfectly natural punishment, for it is but the direct effect of the unfitness for the higher grade, of which the offence has furnished the evidence.

Distinction by dress is a bad, an unjust punishment. It is but a peculiarly high degree of dishonor, and every thing urged against the latter, applies therefore in a peculiarly high degree to this. Either an individual is dead to shame, or not; if the first, the punishment has little effect on him, except, perhaps, to awaken, after all, a feeling of sullen revenge or dangerous contempt. If some feeling of honor is left, what can be the effect of totally embittering the soul of the sufferer? It is a moral, protracted torture, to which the state has no right. The punishment is incalculable, and strikes the better ones most, and most injuriously. It alienates, deadens, or inflames. I speak here of civil punition; the privation of certain signs of honor in the army, for instance the field-sign in Prussia, worn by every soldier of good character, and of which he can be deprived by court-martial only, stands on a different ground, and is wise, just and effective. It allows to do away with a number of bad punishments, especially flogging. Yet the recovery of this sign by good or distinguished conduct, ought always to be left open to the offender, as is actually the case in that army. Never shall I forget the degree of proud confidence with which a soldier asked for his field-sign after the assault of Namur, and the unbounded joy with which he received the beloved sign of honor.

Infamation of the offender is every way a bad punishment. Enough, if we are obliged to punish, and yet unable to mete out according to all the bearings of guilt. We cannot weigh the many thousand effects of bad example, disorderly education, pressing distress, peculiar organization. Be satisfied with punishing strictly yet mildly; but do not strike at the moral man himself, and before all do not murder in him the only thing left, by which he may, perhaps, be rescued, rescue himself. If reform, wherever it is possible, be one of the best preventives of crime, why prevent it most effectually by declaration of infamy, by saying, "thou art a villain, and shalt remain such forever." We have seen that punishment is necessary, for the offender, for society at large, for every thing that is sacred in man; but beyond this I ask who has ever made himself acquainted with the history of many offenders and not felt obliged to strike at his own breast in leaving a prison, and to say, "I too might be here?" The state transgresses its proper sphere in infaming, far worse than it would act were it to decree that slow poison should be given to the offender, so that he should linger through a wretched life. As to the infamation of the children and whole generations yet unborn, we say nothing. Strange that men have never punished the ascendants of an offender, but only the descendants. There would be more plausibility, it seems to me, in punishing the father of an offender, than his son; for the father may at least have a share in the offence by the bad education he gave to his offspring.

Pillory.—What shall I say of this punishment? Weak, for the most degraded villain, and a world of torment to the offender who has the slightest feeling left; it actually rises in an inverse ratio with the moral state of the offender. The less hardened the greater the despair. And how does it operate upon the community? It feeds the vilest propensities in its vilest members, delighted in gazing upon a wretch fettered, perhaps curbed and tortured at the same time, by the mighty power of the state. Let us speak frankly: the pillory is an infamous punishment, just fit for a state which forgets its whole dignity, its character, nay its common duty, and sinks to the level of the offender, or below him. Who commits the worst offence, the individual who pretends to pry into futurity and obtains money from the gullible, or the state which inflicts so barbarous a punishment for this offence? The punishment of public exposure is incalculable, both as to the offender and the community, for they may aggravate the punishment or not, by throwing offensive articles at the offender, as so frequently happens. Have you ever seen a man or woman in the pillory, and heard the yelling of the brutal? Have you ever seen a defenceless wretch exposed to nauseous missiles, without feeling your heart boil with indignation? In what light does public authority appear, when it exposes an offender in the pillory and has, at the same time, to appoint police officers in order to protect him against those to whom he is exposed? Oh! it is an unrighteous, immoral, vile punishment; it makes worse, and, God be thanked, that the nature of man is of such organization that it cannot but become worse by such treatment.

Whipping.—I feel myself free of any morbid philanthropy, and cannot see what objection can be made to castigation merely on general grounds; still less can I see why the state should not have a right to whip, as some have denied it, were it a punishment otherwise recommendable. Castigation, if not applied in anger or passion, restricted to that age in which the child must already be trained, because its passions begin strongly to develop themselves, while yet its reasoning powers are incapable of following up any train of thought, and if otherwise properly limited, as every sort of punishment must be, is salutary in domestic punition. Omitting it is in many cases a grave dereliction of duty, and but too frequently the effect of unwillingness to do what is painful to us. Nay more, whatever species of prison discipline we may adopt, cases will present themselves—I own they are rare, yet they do offer themselves—in which we gain the moral conviction that the infliction of stripes would have a sound effect on the offender, and break the way for more important ones, of a more moral character. Yet spite of all these considerations, whipping is, in my opinion, a bad punishment, not to be tolerated in a civilized community, which has the means of building prisons. As to public whipping, nearly every thing that has been said of the pillory, holds likewise respecting this species of punishment, and I may add, all public infliction of pain. The people assembled at such degrading exhibitions are divided into two parts; the one suffer at the sight, and all their feeling turns in favor of the sufferer; the other, yell at seeing a fellow-creature writhe in agony or approve of his manly callousness; in short, in either case the effect on the community by way of example is bad: add the disgusting sight of the blood streaming from the lacerated back, especially when, as some codes decree, for some high offences, the whipping is to be repeated at every corner of the street, or as that inhuman punishment was which Titus Oates suffered in consequence of the sentence passed by Justice Wilkins, though there had been provocation enough.

Whipping within the prison walls may be either the punishment for the offence itself, or intended as disciplinary means of the convict, independent of his sentence. In either case it ought to be given up.

I have already mentioned that most offenders—all who have committed a series of offences—feel themselves at war with society. As long as this feeling continues, no improvement, though it were but the political one of resolving to obey in future the laws of the country, can be hoped for. Fear alone affects the old offender very little, except that he resolves to be more cautious in future. Hope is too closely interwoven with the whole organization of man, that we should not expect the criminal to hope for escape, when actually there are so many chances of escape from condign punishment in the best regulated state. Now a convict, who just comes from the court where sentence has been passed, must be either the most abject slave, or have suddenly turned a saint, were he to bless the whip which inflicts the smarting stripes upon his back. The one is not desirable, the other not to be expected. Pain galls, irritates, exasperates; whipping makes the chasm between the convict and society still wider; he swears vengeance; "he will have out his flogging's worth," as a convict once expressed it to me. Whipping applies to the mere brutal nature of man, and, therefore, brutalizes still more. Whipping, moreover, is not accommodable, it is an infinitely severer punishment to the feeling, than to the callous; or shall we admit the principle that the less educated shall be whipped for offences for which the more fortunate are but to be imprisoned?

It is repugnant to all feeling of justice; and how can the judge find out the precise line in each case? Is education and a higher feeling of honor so graspable a thing, that public authority can lay hold on it, use it as a mark of distinction? In some cases it may be so; in thousands it is certainly not. Besides this it is uncommonly difficult to define and prescribe whipping so as to exclude unjust increase or decrease of the punishment by the one who whips. It cannot be done, and becomes quite impossible if we allow the infliction of stripes as disciplinary means within the prison walls. It is easy to prescribe rules; who can limit the excitement and irritation of the prison officer at a just provocation? who can possibly prevent an ill-humored, harsh or cruel officer—and why should there be no such individuals among them, as among all others—from using harshly and cruelly the whip, if once allowed to him? The Norwegian code, published in 1835, and which, in many respects, breathes the spirit of mildness and humanity, ordains that for common offences within the prison, not more than six strokes, either with a stick of hazel or a rope, shall be inflicted. The stick shall not be thicker than 2 inches in circumference; the rope not tarred, and from 1¾ to 2 inches in circumference, nor longer than a yard. The prisoner shall not undress, nor be tied. Should he defend himself the proper authority can decree more stripes. Under these latter and other circumstances, specified in the code, the prisoner shall be tied with a wide thong round the loins, to a post, covered with a stuffed bag, so that it forms a soft cylinder. The arms are to be tied round the post, and the stripes are to be inflicted between the shoulders, alternately by two persons, at intervals of ten seconds. The intention of the lawgiver in being so minute cannot be mistaken, but alas! a man must know little of prison affairs not to know that this punishment might yet be executed with ferocious cruelty or lenient partiality. And who is the superintendent over the faithful execution of this law? Will you listen to complaints of the convicts? They will tell you more than you could ever listen to. Will you trust the prison officer alone? Trust no one, not yourself, with the whip in the hand, when provoked to punish. That each whipping interferes with the due effect of imprisonment, i. e. to make a good impression, no challenging one, is evident. It is cheering, therefore, to observe that flogging has steadily diminished with the advance of civilization; many armies exist without flogging;* and from some codes it is stricken altogether. We have to congratulate ourselves on seeing it abolished in Bavaria. At least the papers have stated that the Bavarian chambers had voted its discontinuance in 1837.

Branding is brutal, and has all the ill effects of infamation, indelibly stamped on the culprit. Let us treat penologic matters plainly and simply. What, I ask, can a man feel, according to human nature, whether guilty or not, whom we have branded in the hand or on the forehead? Shall we expect wonders of a convict, or simply expect effects of the causes as our nature must teach us to be prepared for them. You tell him he is a wild beast; you stamp him as a wild beast. Well then, expect that he continues forever to act as such. You outlaw a man, for branding is more than outlawing, it is thrusting him out of the very pale of human society—and then expect or at least wish for a compliance with the laws, on his part.

Infliction of pain in public is objectionable on all the grounds on which I have declared myself against public whipping.

Imprisonment.—All civilized nations are agreed that privation of personal liberty is the best punishment for the greater number of offences, and the more a nation advances in civilization and penologic knowledge, the more it strives to develop its prison system according to experience, justice and humanity. As I shall give my views on this species of punition more fully, I may leave the subject for the present.

Imprisonment with public labor, e. g. in the streets or on the highways, is bad on account of the various reasons already given. It operates exceedingly unevenly. I have seen an elderly man in chains working on the high road because he had

* Lord William Bentinck, when Governor General of India, abolished, in February 1835, the flogging of native soldiers at all the Presidencies.

sold some wood belonging to the crown forests, for his own account. I was told, that it was his only offence. He was there with other offenders, who showed their utter callousness by their language toward each other, and their harassing treatment of the elderly man, who had been an officer of considerable rank. He had the insane look of despair. All public exposure of convicts is inadmissible by penology. It deadens, makes callous, and renders worse. It operates badly on the offender and the community. How can, by possibility, an individual, who has dragged his heavy chain for ten years through the streets of a fortress, be expected to live honestly ever after? On account of fear? Not so; when man fears he tries to evade or obviate the object of fear, and yet follows his inclination. And does the community, among whom he is known as the long degraded convict who had hardly a single opportunity to reform, allow him to live honestly? If ever society—I do not say governments, for it is futile to declaim against governments, in cases in which they do nothing but act out the spirit of society—if ever society have committed crimes, it was when those long chains, to which a large number of convicts were fettered, young and old, high and low, first offenders and hardened criminals, unfortunate and desperate, all on one chain were led from Paris or other coast towns to the Bagnes, in France. This iniquity is happily abolished. It was not in France alone the case.

In the Motives of the Plan of a Penal Code for the Kingdom of Wurtemberg, (Stuttgardt 1836,) we find (add. art. 11,) the following:

"It is evident that a punishment, according to which the convict is obliged to work in a distinctive dress before the eyes of the public, must be much severer for him in whom all feeling of shame is not yet dead.

"If the judge were allowed to pronounce with his sentence to imprisonment, likewise condemnation to public labor, a great disproportion among the convicts, according to their degree of morality and individuality, would arise." (The punishment would not be accommodable.)....... "Against this demand of justice, the pecuniary advantage of the prison is of no importance, especially since it appears certain that public labor, which affects the feeling of honor so deeply, operates against one of the objects of punishment, never to be lost sight of—the reform of the criminal. These were the reasons why it was considered improper to leave it to the judge to connect with his sentence to imprisonment likewise that to public labor. As, however, those more delicate regards are of no avail with such convicts as have been accustomed to labor in the open air, from their early youth, who prefer it to that in a confined space, nay, as experience teaches, request it as a favor, no reason could be found not to *permit* public labor, if the convict desires it."

All contained in this passage is just, with the exception of two things. First, a person may have been accustomed to labor in the open field and yet feel ashamed to do it as a convict. Yet the choice is left him: this too is highly objectionable; for, not to speak of the indirect means, always at the disposal of a prison officer to make a convict do certain things, whether he has the right to force him or not, society demands that the prisoner be not exposed, because it is known that he cannot be reformed if he is, and society has the greatest interest in seeing all fair means tried to induce him not to offend in future. The state becomes in a great degree the guardian of the prisoner, and has no right to expose him to public gaze, though he should desire it and should actually feel physically the better for it.

Exile, if applied to political offenders, is an apt punishment, otherwise it is inhuman to turn criminals upon other states. A few years ago a vessel from Europe brought a number of criminals, actually sentenced to the United States. The less our authorities were able to act against them, according to our laws, the more atrocious was it in the foreign authority to turn these criminals upon a distant community. Among the offenders were some who had committed arson!

Transportation is a species of punishment which can be made use of but by few communities, on account of its expensiveness. There are besides grave considerations in the way;

if the criminals are comparatively free in the colony, the punishment is very slight for the hardened and very severe for the reformable convict; for he has to live in a debased community, made up of the scum of society; becomes closely allied with them, and finds himself, on his return, a member of the society of rogues, which keeps him within its meshes wherever he goes.

Maiming is worse than all public punishments we have mentioned, for it adds still greater barbarity to the punishment, prevents reform still more effectually, actually deprives in some cases, of the possibility of earning a livelihood, debases society by accustoming it to barbarous sights, prevents punishment, because the judge hesitates to pronounce sentence, so shocking to all better feelings, and, therefore, promotes crime, and ruins the offender irredeemably. To cut the ears, split the nose, &c., are punishments which have come down to us from times when the effecting of bodily fear was the only object of punishment.

Death.—I do not wish to give here my opinion on capital punishment; not that I have not made up my mind with regard to it, or that I would hesitate one moment frankly to state my thoughts, but I should wish to give connectedly all my reasons on so grave a subject, on which many untenable arguments have been urged on both sides; and for this an opportunity will not be wanting. As to death with additional pains or infamatory procedures, it must be considered as entirely inadmissible. These additions have no other effect whatever than engaging all sympathy for the criminal and turning it against the penal authority; of affording greater opportunity of escape to those whose crimes, according to the law, would have merited this severer punishment, than to those who have committed a less offence, so that actually criminals have been glad when they found that their indictment was for the most heinous crimes; it has a baneful effect upon the gazing multitude, and even those that merely read the laws or hear of them, and can of course have no moral effect upon the criminal, while, surely, he who is not prevented from committing crime by fear that discovery will lead to the scaffold, would not be more so by the fear of a painful death. The only consideration, which might warrant increased pain, could be, that public morality demands a scale of punishment, and that it is offending it not to punish the interested parricide, or the slow poisoner, more severely than the wrathful murderer. The answer is, that, though this was undoubtedly one of the guiding principles in former times, we shall always be obliged to stop somewhere; some punishment we must acknowledge as the ultimum supplicium, and that we injure much and benefit no one by modified punishments of death. It is for ever bad if the state appears as tormentor.

Of all the desirable or necessary qualities which punishment ought to possess none unites so many as imprisonment, though there are likewise the most serious objections to be made against it, if it is not managed with great wisdom. The advantages of imprisonment have always been, its graduableness, its controllableness, and the fact that the state, in applying it, appears in a less ferocious or a more dignified character: the punishment is calm in its nature. Imprisonment, moreover, punishes without exposure to public gaze, and has thus been often used with the higher classes, in cases in which bodily chastisement would have been inflicted with individuals of the lower orders. A community which introduces imprisonment is always making a step forward in civilization. The serious objections to imprisonment were increased expense, because the prisoner must be supported by the state, and baneful associations and intercourse among the imprisoned.

Whenever two individuals, whose prominent actions have been produced or strongly affected by the same vital impulse, come in contact, they impel one another in their career with still greater force and rapidity. It is the law of all intercourse. If the brave meets with the brave, the adventurer with the adventurer, the devout with the devout, the student with the student, the patriotic with the patriotic, the artist with the artist, the debauched with the debauched, the miser with the miser, the foppish with the foppish, the criminal with the criminal, the vital element of their respective actions will be increased in intensity by their intercourse. If you bring two evil-disposed persons, especially two individuals whose presence in the prison points out crime as a prominent feature in their life, in close contact, and if in both there was before the contact a certain and equal degree of criminality, this criminality will have greatly increased after the contact, because, as I stated, they, as all other men, good or bad, will propel each other in that line, which is characteristically their own. This increases where there are more than two brought in contact; not only that the less criminal will be attracted by the more criminal, but even the most criminal of the company will gain in criminality by the mutual contact. Add to this the common principles of so many human actions, reluctance to acknowledge wrong, pride in resisting force, opposition to our real or misconceived enemy, readiness to seize upon arguments which promise to overbalance a consciousness, however dim it may be, of our wrong, a desire to chace out of the memory the images of those who once gave good counsel, which will now and then rise like summoning ghosts, and finally, the degree of acute attention which is paid to the counsels of prudence, which promise to furnish means of escaping in future that evil under which we suffer in the present moment—and it is easy enough to understand *a priori* what experience, without a single exception, proves with frightful facts, that nothing can be more baneful to criminals than their close intercourse with one another, freed as it is, in prison, from all those intervening occupations and distractions which the variegated life out of the walls of the prison always must offer. The prisoner shows to his fellow-prisoner by the fact that they meet in that place, that crime has brought him there; as criminals they meet, and as criminals they commune with one another. It is this baneful effect of intercourse which in penology is called contamination—an effect which, however easy to understand on general psychologic grounds, nevertheless far outstrips all imagination of the virtuous who have not made prison matters a specific object of study—an effect from which no prisoner can escape, because it takes place according to the first principles of human nature, common to all the good as well as the wicked, and to which the state has, therefore, no right to expose. The state says: "thou hast offended, I must punish." We grant the right, but the state has no right to corrupt, and it does corrupt positively, directly and not accidentally, because the corruption takes place as a necessary consequence of joint imprisonment, according to the nature of man, which the state has neither the power nor the right to change. The state has no right to corrupt; the prisoner can claim it, and ought to claim it, were he awake to his true rights and interests, and society claims it, because it demands to be protected against crime, not to have it increased tenfold by wicked carelessness on the part of the state. What should we say of a teacher, who, in order to punish inattention, should choose a punishment by which necessarily and unavoidably inattention is increased, for instance, by placing the boy so that he may amuse himself by looking at a military parade? The least we could say would be, that he is a foolish teacher. Contamination, therefore, making the criminal still worse than he is, is to be avoided. Let us rightly understand the matter: it is not a demand made on the score of charity, still less of overstrained philanthropy; it is a demand founded on the strictest right. The state which exposes to contamination, after having become acquainted with the fact, acts criminally if it persist, frequently more criminally than the offender, who may have been led to his offence by want, by utterly neglected education, by bad laws of the state itself. The state becomes the wilful perpetuator of crime, and, inasmuch as it frustrates the intended effect of its punishments, a cruel offender itself, because it inflicts suffering (the punishment) for no purpose: it becomes, lastly, the heedless squanderer of enormous sums, which the administration of penal justice requires—the annual budget of crime, as Mr. Quetelet so justly calls it—because it does not repress crime, but actually generates it, nurses it in hot beds, diligently taking care that no seed should be lost, but each one should thrive in the freest possible luxuriance. Though I use similes,

I speak but of plain truth, as you, Sir, and every one acquainted with prison matters, well know.

Separation, then, becomes necessary. The sexes were early separated; but not even these always. At a later period classification was adopted; the young were separated from the old; farther divisions were made according to sentences. The actually tried crime, and consequent sentence became the standard. It is a standard, and better than none, but it is nevertheless an inefficient one; for who does not know that a convict, sentenced but for a short time for theft, may be infinitely more guilty at heart, and, therefore, far more dangerous on the score of contamination, than another who has been committed, perhaps for maiming, for a far longer period? Here it becomes important to observe what I have alluded to above, that state and society, though they have their distinct manifestations, still remain closely linked together, and we shall be strangely misled every time we attempt to sever them, and to make the state act on its own abstract principles as if society were not in existence, while the state is, in truth, its shield and protection. On the one hand the state must needs exist; the state is an institution founded on right, cemented by law; it must uphold the law, and cannot, dare not, enter into the mere morality of the individual. The fact—the deed, is the only thing to go by. On the other hand, it is harsh to punish the less guilty more severely than the more criminal offender, and nowise to pay attention to this fact; to right again, if I may say so, this necessary disproportion as much as possible. We know we must punish conformably to facts, and not dispositions; but we likewise know that the tried misdeed was, perhaps, but the effect of accident; that the thief would have committed cold-blooded murder, had he thought it necessary, and that the murderer never would have thought of his bloody deed, had he not been provoked to the quick. How are all these difficulties to be adjusted?

There are yet many other classifications, not made by unprofitable analysis, but on the nature of criminals. First there are young transgressors, who have offended because never submitted to sound and strict discipline: secondly, offenders who commit infractions of the law rather from an absence of principles, than the presence of settled bad principles, from thoughtlessness, rather than positive, deeply rooted and conscious perversity: thirdly, hardened, reflecting criminals. Again, there are offenders in whom shame, that nucleus of possible reform, is not annihilated; others who have lost it. There are offenders who have transgressed the laws from sheer heedlessness, others from rashness, others again who are criminals by trade, well trained in thought and skill. How is it possible to make all these classifications in reality? How can we make the necessary subdivisions according to all the various shades and combinations? How can we test the real state of an offender—and this would be absolutely necessary; for as soon as sentence according to strict law or fact has been passed, it is for society to step in again and treat every case according to its moral demerits as far as lies in human power? How after all, can we prevent contamination, even after the subtlest classification? Yet it stands firm as one of the first principles of all punition: "the state has no particle of right to make worse, to promote criminality." By no other earthly means is this possible than by treating each case singly—by insulation of each prisoner.

The necessity of insulation has frequently occurred to penetrating minds. It is so well founded in human nature that I have little doubt but that we would meet with it after some historical search at a very early date. In fact we know that it was frequently adopted in monastic punition; and the venerable and celebrated father Mabillon, (who died in 1707,) who wrote on the moral reform of the prisons of his order, the Benedictines, actually lays down uninterrupted solitude, labor, silence, and prayer as the four principles on which the offenders of his order ought to be imprisoned. He advises solitary cells and uninterrupted confinement. I follow, in this statement, a passage of his works,* given in the introduction to Moreau-

* Posthumous Works, ed. of 1724, vol. II. p. 321 and seq. I quote after the above work.

Cristophe's Actual State of the Prisons in France, Paris, 1837; and have mentioned it, not in order to show that solitary confinement at labor is strictly a French invention, as the author says, but that it is one of those natural things to which the mind of man must have been led at various times and in various places.

All penologists of note—I do not speak of those few lawyers who view the subject merely as judges, I had almost said, for whom the criminal loses all interest as soon as the case is decided and offers no more legal difficulties, or who think that they know much of the peculiar compound character of a criminal, because they have passed sentence on many, while in fact they know the criminal only with the lawyer by his side—all penologists of note, I say, are agreed on this point, that insulation of the criminal is the only possible means: 1. To avoid contamination: 2. To effect reform, if reform be possible. In the most different quarters of the globe we see it adopted, wherever a reform of prison systems takes place with civilized nations. No difficulty exists as to the principle, but men are not so well agreed as to its execution. We, the advocates of uninterrupted confinement at labor, say nothing short of actual, material insulation is sufficient: the advocates of the Auburn system say all the necessary effects of insulation can be obtained by actual separation during night, and joint labor in silence by day, while the former offers many evils and the latter several advantages.

I intend to state the important advantages which we believe are to be derived from our system, its disadvantages, and then to consider the objections made by the advocates of the Auburn system; finally to show what we conceive to be the unavoidable disadvantages of the Auburn system.

We conceive uninterrupted solitude and labor of equal importance, for the following reasons:

1. It prevents effectually contamination, and it alone can effectually prevent it. It allows, therefore, the offender, at any rate, not to grow worse.

2. It is essentially both a stern and a humane punishment;

stern, because solitude is stern in its character and especially so to men, who nearly without exception have spent their lives in boisterous intercourse with fellow criminals; and humane, because it is a privation rather than an infliction. It is mild, and acknowledged as such by the offenders themselves after the first irksomeness of solitude has passed, especially if they have passed previously through several other prisons or penitentiaries. Whomever of this class I have known, has voluntarily confessed it, while frequently their eyes would flash with resentment when they spoke of penitentiaries founded on other plans. Solitary confinement at labor is decidedly a calm punishment.

3. It is emphatically graduable and accommodable as no other species of punishment. The offender, undisturbed by others, or by new inflictions of punishment, receives from solitude just that impression which his peculiar case or disposition calls for or is capable of.

4. Advice and exhortation can be adapted to each single case in no other punishment, so precisely and justly like moral medicine, as in solitary confinement. The religious adviser, assistant and comforter can enter the solitary cell at any time, and, as all religious conversations with a convict must have much of the character of a confession, the undisturbed cell, overheard by no one, is the very place for this converse. In no other penitentiaries can this religious instruction be given so effectually.

5. Solitude is the weightiest moral agent to make the thoughtless thoughtful—to reflect, and the only one sufficiently powerful for the criminally thoughtless. Solitude has been sought by the wisest and best of mankind, to prepare themselves for great moral tasks; it is the only means to bring the offender to a more rational course. Labor united with solitude gives steadiness to the thought, and makes it possible to support solitude with ease for those who have not been accustomed to abstract reflection before.

6. It is the only punishment known, which does not irritate anew, does not challenge opposition in mind or body; for it is

the only punishment which can dispense with the whip or other means of coercing to obedience, because it takes away the opportunity of offending anew, with the exception of such offences as destroying instruments or materials, for which again the more negative disciplinary means of withholding labor or diminishing rations are sufficient.

7. It makes the lonely prisoner love labor as faithfully as the dearest companion—a companion who will be with him for life.

8. It does not deaden shame by exposure; on the contrary, it shames many into repentance by its absence of all harshness, as I frequently have found. It does not inflict on those who have a strong sense of shame, the additional punishment of exposure.

9. It does not expose the convict to acquaintance, even by night, with other criminals, who out of the prison form a very compact fraternity, to escape from the clutches of which forms the most difficult obstacle in the way of resuming an honest life. The history of innumerable convicts proves this. Whenever I have asked recommitted convicts why, simply on the score of worldly prudence, they had not abstained from a second crime, they would invariably answer: "You do not know these things; a man leaving the prison, very often thinks, you shall not catch me again. He begins to work, when old acquaintances will come, induce one to drink and talk, and all will end by agreeing upon a new job. If one resists, he is ridiculed, or threatened with exposure." No tiger's fang is so firmly buried in his victim's flesh, as that of criminal acquaintance in the life of an offender.

10. It contradicts for the first time, by irresistible fact, the convicts in their belief that society is at war with them, in which they please themselves so much, that frequently they argue as if they were the hunted, the pursued, the injured.

11. The punishment has, therefore, what I have called an elevating character. It touches the man in the convict, not the brute. The convict sees himself treated as one on whom far different things than stripes can have an effect.

12. It is, perhaps, the only punishment which allows us to select men for superintendents of prisons in whom sternness does not overbalance kindness.

13. It trains the convict in cleanliness, and paying attention to the neatness of his dwelling; it imparts an attention to the room, which becomes the incipient stage of love of home, with those who have lived in slouchy disregard of it. It is an old English saying, full of meaning, "cleanliness is next to godliness." A strictly cleanly man of the laboring classes will never be so much exposed to offend against the laws, as a disorderly, dirty person. Cleanliness, a highly important ingredient of national civilization, is equally such in political reform.

14. All the reasons given in favor of the Pennsylvania plan assume still higher importance with the youthful or first offenders, because their minds are yet more ready to receive good impressions, and they have not yet formed that vast association with criminals of older standing. I was once present when a convict was brought to be entered in the Philadelphia penitentiary. His age—he was past forty, and the peculiar manner with which he spoke of his mode of life, which cannot be designated precisely as frivolity, but rather professional indifference, attracted my attention. He had been seventeen years of his life in prison, never before in a penitentiary on the Pennsylvania plan, and I chose him as an experiment to observe the effect of solitary confinement on an old offender, who "had lived in various lines, but always in that trade," as his words were. I cannot give here an extract of my journal respecting him, but will merely mention that John—this was his name—after having treated lightly the confinement, and not having changed for a long time to speak with frankness indeed, but also with perfect unconcern of his "trade," and the various lines in which the different nations excel, one day said to me of his own accord, and with more gravity than I had been accustomed to observe with him: "Sir, what will become of me I don't know. To be sure, I now think it foolish enough to live as I have done; but I do not know how it will be when I get out. I am accustomed to nothing else. But, Sir, had

they put me here when I committed my first offence, I know for certain I should not be here now."

15. It appears to me a great advantage of the Pennsylvania system that the prisoner is not prevented, by false shame, from lending his ear to better counsel, and gradually changing for the better. Wherever a number of men live together in close community under some superiors, a degree of fear exists of being considered by their comrades as a peculiar favorite of those placed over them on account of stricter compliance with the respective laws and rules. We find this in schools, colleges, among soldiers, sailors, &c. The individual does not wish to be suspected of using unfair means, or being an informer, in order to obtain this favor, and this well founded feeling leads generally to the excess I have alluded to. In a community, however, in which a ready compliance with the rules of the superiors becomes, in a manner, a reproach to the others, a joining of the opposite party as it were, a declaration of the intention to abandon in future those who, until then, have been associates, it requires far more resolution and moral character to brave the sneers of former comrades and, perhaps, own false shame of declaring one's self ready to surrender. The apprehension of a nickname is one of the most powerful agents in any community; but how easily is such a nickname, a taunt, a word of contempt, passed on in the lockstep of the Auburn system. All this difficulty is happily removed in our system; no false shame awaits the convict when he shows the first signs of sorrow, when he utters his first acknowledgment of guilt or folly; at least no shame of appearing weak before comrades in guilt, which is far more powerful than that of surrendering to those whom the prisoner almost always allows to be better, with the same readiness with which a prostitute will always speak of other women as virtuous ones.

16. The convict thinks in kindness of his keepers, and the memory of the penitentiary is not a galling sore, when he has left it, and chooses to live by his labor.

17. This system depends less upon the skill of the officers, or a long apprenticeship, than the Auburn system, in order to

make it answer at all. The Pennsylvania system, therefore, is easier to be introduced.

18. It is sufficient with our race and at the stage of civilization we are now in, and no more, which is what a punishment ought to be. This point, which by experience alone, i. e. by close and circumspect observation of reality, not by hasty numbers and rash conclusions, can be decided, appears so to us; and none of us has seen reason as yet to change his opinion.

19. Finally, it offers the greatest security, being in this superior to all other species of imprisonment.

The disadvantages of this system are, as far as I am able to penetrate the subject, not of a moral or essential character, but merely accidental.

1. The greater expense of building the prison. I allow a penitentiary on our plan is more expensive, but we must not forget three points—that if we succeed in preventing crime from extending through the state, it is cheap after all. People are unwilling to calculate the enormous loss of property and labor first caused by crime itself, and then the great expense of punishing it. Secondly, that the latest penitentiaries on the Pennsylvania plan (built by Mr. Haviland) are much cheaper than the first, when experience had not yet been collected. Thirdly, that if penitentiaries on the Auburn plan shall have any effect at all, they ought never to contain more than about 300 prisoners. The farther you go beyond this number the more you stand in need of inexorable sternness and uninterrupted fear on the part of the convicts, to keep such a colossus properly subdued. Mr. Pilsbury, the very intelligent and experienced superintendent of the Wethersfield penitentiary—he has been for twelve years prison officer, and has inherited, as it were, considerable experience from his father, who was likewise prison officer—lately said to me, that there ought not to be more than 300 to 350 convicts in one penitentiary: 400 he considers as the very utmost. Our penitentiaries may be indefinitely increased; for the number of prisoners changes nothing, does not increase danger. If with the increased number of convicts, the number

of moral physicians is increased, nothing is changed in the matter. So that actually the difference of cost would nearly vanish.

2. Many profitable species of labor cannot be pursued with us, because they cannot be carried on within doors, or they require joint labor. Be it so; penitentiaries are not erected to make money, but to punish, and, if possible, to reform by the punishment. One point, however, is to be considered—that in the same degree as a species of labor requires the joint exertion of many hands, in precisely the same degree it breaks in upon the original principle of insulation, gives opportunity of contamination and requires increased strictness and severity to avert danger. Is then the loss on our side, because we cannot cut stones, carry on coopering or make blacksmiths? In one respect alone is this limited choice of occupation for the convicts to be regretted, namely, for their future life. It may at times be easier for a blacksmith to find work than for a shoemaker, but what is this even problematic advantage against all the disadvantage resulting from joint labor? Shall we give up the very principle upon which the whole is founded in order to obtain one not important advantage? Should we thus infringe the fundamental principle for an entirely extraneous consideration, while everywhere this principle is carried out more and more; while in France convicts are now carried to their places of punishment in cellular carriages, in which communication is prevented?*

* The following is from a Paris paper of October 1837.

"We borrow from a contemporary the following account of the new cellular carriages for the conveyance of convicts to the ports and places of confinement. Each carriage is formed into twelve compartments, six on each side, with a passage in the middle. In each of the cells is a bench, on which the prisoner sits with his face to the horses; the seat, which may be converted into a chaise percée, is wadded, as well as the sides of the cell. In front of the prisoner is a pocket for his provisions, which are put in at the door. Air and light are admitted from the top, so that the men inclosed can see no external object. The prisoners have irons on their legs, but the rest of their bodies are free, and they may change their position at will, but they are strictly forbidden to speak. Two guards are placed in

The objections made by those who prefer the Auburn system, few as they are now, may be comprehended, as far as I have ascertained them, under the following heads:

1. We have no right to condemn a human being to uninterrupted solitude. The same objection was made to insulation in general, when the penitentiary system attracted closer attention. Much was said about inalienable rights, refined cruelty under the garb of humanity, exaction of things which go directly against the nature implanted by the Creator in our inmost soul, and the like. Inalienable rights are very excellent things if rightly understood, but great bugbears if handled by superficial minds, who feel rather than reason, and whose feeling again is the result of early, sometimes accidental impressions rather than the effect of a well-schooled heart; but the human heart requires as much schooling as the head. No man will deny that the right of utterance is a most sacred one, an inalienable right; but does inalienable right mean that which we have at any time a right to practice? Then, who has given those a right to punish me, who would certainly do so, were I to stand up in a church and converse with the minister in a pulpit? Who has a right to exact silence of me in a legislative hall, if I am not a member of the body? How can a general prohibit talking, by pain of death, during a hazardous expedition at night, upon which the safety of the army, of a country, may depend? What right can be more inalienable than that of locomotion? Yet am I allowed to locomove wherever I choose, into the garden, the house, the closet of my neighbor? It is futile indeed to talk about the absence of right of preventing people from talking. The only question can be, can you exact it? is the object you obtain by it equivalent to the violence necessary to counteract the natural, and in general, salutary disposition of communion? With peculiarly bad grace, however, does this charge come from the advocates of the Auburn system—not from all, indeed; in fact, not from one, as far as I

---

the passage, and thus have the convicts constantly under their superintendence. These carriages travel night and day, and require six horses each."

know, who knows something practically about these matters, and views them so. I have never heard the charge made by wardens or superintendents, but have seen it in writings by such who showed otherwise that they were utterly unacquainted with the subject, or that they persisted in repeating hundredfold refuted charges, because they chose to do so. Have we no right to imprison a man in a spacious, cleanly and airy cell, with a yard attached to it, and yet are called upon to admit the right of allowing hundreds of men to walk, work and live together without daring to open their mouths, and of locking them up at night or Sundays in narrow, gloomy cells, tortured by the desire to talk to the neighbor with whom, according to the locality, conversation might be had, but must not be had? The demand is absolutely preposterous.

2. *Loneliness.*—Under this head several charges are made, and some which it is very painful to answer, for they are so puerile in their character, that a man who sees the grave importance of the subject, feels humbled while he answers them; yet if they are not answered, he who had the boldness first to start them feels strengthened by repetition, and after long repetition people are found who will believe them—a circumstance which is far more dangerous in penologic matters, than in others. If ever there was a subject on which it is easier to say plausible yet radically wrong things, nay to start and insist upon dicta which have an insinuating appearance for the multitude and yet are recognised at once by the penologist as sheer nonsense, that subject is penology, for the simple reason that the public at large happily are, and must be as long as there are far more honest men than rogues, utterly unacquainted with the peculiar compound of which the character of a criminal consists. They are far better than many believe, far more corrupt than others think, and what is more important, their character is not to be treated, not to be seized upon by the same means, only stronger, which influence daily the morally healthy ones.

I have been led to these remarks, by the fact of having seen it stated in print—and I was informed that it came from no scurrilous source—that the Pennsylvania system is objectionable because "it is not good that man should be alone." I frankly ask every open-hearted man—for or against our system, it matters not, whether a man of candor must not feel disgusted to write on such unworthy, aye! unrighteous application of the bible? Is it meant that as in that passage of Genesis *alone* signifies the state without a wife, for it reads: "And the Lord God said, it is not good that the man should be alone: I will make him an help meet for him," we should not leave the criminals without women? Surely it is not good that man should be alone, but it is still less good for him to be a criminal, to contaminate others by vile words. Surely it is not good to be alone, but it is still less good to be whipped. Surely it is not good to be alone, for ever, but it is an excellent thing to be alone, under certain circumstances, even for good, even for the best men. Let these men who plume their writings with garbled passages of the bible, read Archbishop Whateley's excellent passage on the unholy, irreligious fashion of drawing the bible—the code of religion—into discussions to be decided on philosophic, practical or scientific grounds. We have to draw from the bible the principles which must guide us—in our case that of honoring man even in the criminal, and of shunning no labor to reclaim him—but as to the execution, the application of them, it is silent, or it could not be a book of all times. The bible teaches us to be charitable to the poor, but we have to learn from political economy or from any other quarter, how to be so, without doing it either ineffectually or causing effects still worse than poverty. What, if I were to quote, by way of effect, the passage which teaches us not only not to whip, but meekly to offer one cheek to him who has smitten the other, against the whipping in the Auburn penitentiaries? *I* would be ashamed of doing it.

The other charge under the head of loneliness is, that solitude drives to despair. It was predicted, when uninterrupted solitude was first introduced, that it would lead to insanity, though the trial in the worst shapes had frequently been made before. There have ever been some men in perpetual solitary confinement, even without labor, without becoming insane. When it was proved that it did not lead to insanity; when most unfounded charges, brought against the Pennsylvania system, were proved to be such, some men still continued to insist upon the charge, for what reason is neither necessary nor profitable to investigate here, only so much is evident, that they do not insist upon them from a love of truth. They have facts long and incontestably proven to found their opinion upon, should they choose to do so. What shall I say of such disingenuous hints as are contained in the passage quoted at the beginning from the last Report of the Boston Prison Society? Because two convicts have committed suicide, it is the system which produced it? Shall we count all the suicides committed in the Auburn prisons, and is suicide a rare occurrence in any prison system? Can it be, among men who have lived so melancholy a life, and frequently reflect with bitter anguish or reckless impatience on it? The writer of the passage hints at these suicides, but does he not know that hinting, putting mysterious questions in all matters of a serious kind is far worse than candidly and promptly speaking out—a remark to which I am not led by this passage alone, but because the hinting is common in the style of the writer who composes the leading parts of those Reports. Yet it appears that the suicides are hinted at not as having originated from the lonely cell in general, but chiefly so from the loneliness of the cell on the sabbath. "The solitary cell of a prison is a deadly place to put a man in to spend his sabbaths." Why it is more deadly on sabbaths than any other day I cannot comprehend. But I dismiss the subject for the present, because I have first to answer the other charge against loneliness. It is, that it makes the spirits droop, and injures the health of the convict. Either we go by experience or by notions. We prefer to go by the former; and our per centage of sickness and deaths, as reported by the official physicians, exhibit no such inroads upon the health of the convicts;* many who arrive diseased and broken

* The number of deaths in the Eastern State Penitentiary, Philadelphia, has been as follows:

down recover: and, before all, go and see and talk to them. They do not complain of ill health; they have appetite, and sleep well. And do all the reports of the various committees, appointed year after year by the legislature of Pennsylvania to inquire into the penitentiaries, go for nothing? Is there no reliance to be placed upon the statements of men selected from the highest body of the state, if they uniformly assert, that they are satisfied with the health of the convicts? Are their reports, drawn up with care and published before the whole people, entitled to no belief? Yet they express the most explicit satisfaction on this important point. The legislature of Pennsylvania now assembled have sent more committees, perhaps, than has been the case at any previous period, to examine into the prisons of the state, and their reports, lately printed, do not only give the best account of the state of health in the penitentiaries and jails on the Pennsylvania plan, but they are likewise, in a general point of view, of a character to cheer the friends of our system; for they urgently recommend its introduction into all parts of the state. It seems to me that this fact deserves some attention. Solitary confinement at labor has now been tried for a series of years, during which it has been assailed by the well meaning and ill meaning, with plausible and unfair arguments, in a manner that at various times the legislature deemed it expedient to institute inquiries as to certain specific charges. No argument has been left untried to attack the system, from the want of pecuniary profit, to the accusation that we make madmen of our prisoners; from the alleged interference with the honest mechanic, by underselling

---

1829,	none.	
1830,	3 per cent.	
1831,	6 "	"
1832,	4.4 "	"
1833,	0.8 "	"
1834,	2.7 "	"
1835,	2.6 "	"
1836,	3.3 "	"
1837,	4.4 "	"

him, to the charge of specific cruelty or of our rendering the solitary convict worse and worse by leaving him alone with his corrupted, wicked self; and yet, spite of all these assaults by word and pen, in paper, pamphlet and periodical, we receive one official report after another from men who have no earthly interest in the maintenance of this system beyond that of upright citizens in all good institutions, not only approving of the system as far as introduced, but urging its further adoption to the total exclusion of any other prison system. Shall we believe our own eyes and these official reports, or imputations which come from a distance? Sir, the ignorance respecting our system in our own country is almost inconceivable. Even well disposed though inexcusably imprudent persons speak, nay write on the Pennsylvania system without having any definite idea, still less practical knowledge of its essential principles and mode of operation. Let me state to you a fact. The excellent superintendent of one of the best conducted houses of refuge, founded in a neighboring city of Philadelphia, was astonished when I told him that the convicts in the Philadelphia penitentiary work in their cells. He had believed that they were imprisoned without labor. You ask, when did this happen? supposing, probably, that this must have been at the earliest period of our system. It was as late as the year 1833. As to other persons, unconnected with prisons in any way, the vagueness of ideas is of course still greater. Frequently have I heard exclamations at the cruelty of solitary imprisonment, commiseration for the poor convict, when a brief explanation would suffice to show that it is cruelty to throw him into a pool of vice by imprisoning him with others, but not, to protect him by solitary confinement.

The dispute would be much shorter if we were told that no fact should weigh, no reason convince. But as long as this is not done, we have a claim to see facts properly weighed and acknowledged. Loneliness, it is said, will do little good to the criminal, whose diseased fancy will rove in regions far from those whence reform should come. There is truth in this, but our sort of confinement makes the visits of the advising friend and teacher much easier than in the Auburn prisons, where the minister must call them from their labor in order to speak to them, which is very inconvenient, or he must speak to them in those narrow cells, or through the grate in the door! How is it possible to be of much use in such a way; to gain the confidence and effect that degree of ease, communion and confidence without which the conversation with the convict must be greatly deprived of its intended effect.

The last objection is that we cannot celebrate the sabbath.—I should have spoken of this subject under the charges which we make against the Auburn system—namely, Sunday congregations—but for the fact, that it is not necessarily connected with that system, though I think that instruction which can be given in the exceedingly narrow cells of the Auburn penitentiaries, being overheard by others, must be very deficient.

It is said then, and repeatedly so, that our system is *unnatural*, because it admits of no sabbath worship. I ask why? Are we pagans, that our worship is necessarily bound to certain rites? Is it enjoined by the founder of our religion to celebrate the sabbath precisely in a particular form? is a passage to be found which states that christians must publicly, congregatedly worship, in order to worship at all? Public worship, worship in congregated masses, has been acknowledged at all times and by all nations as a means of religious elevation, and of peculiar edification. It does the heart good to bow down before the Almighty, with a number of fellow-creatures; but if evils arise out of public worship greater than the advantage to be derived, we omit it. At all times when plague, or peculiarly malignant diseases of a contagious character, have prevailed, public worship has justly been discontinued, and even prohibited by authority. Did they act "unnaturally?" We object to public worship in penitentiaries most decidedly on these grounds: it makes the convicts acquainted with each other by sight, and fastens, therefore, each one tighter to his criminal career; it sets the ingenuity of the convict to work, to find out how he can possibly make use of the congregation to commune with his neighbor: (all individuals who have been in Auburn penitentiaries, with whom I have conversed, have acknowledged this:) it does not allow the prisoner to put his mind in that frame, which would be required for the true benefit of public worship, because he sees his keepers close at hand, watching him strictly; and lastly, it is of little use to the convict. The moral cares of the convict are of infinite variety, and require special treatment. The same food is good for thousands of healthy persons; all take the same or similar nourishment, but medicine must be mixed and weighed out, singly for each single patient. Farther, what characterizes public worship from private? Instruction? By no means; that can be given in private. It is the general feeling of devotion, heightened by the fact, that many people congregate to adore their maker, and for that, the convict is especially dead in a thousand cases against one. The convict is either stupid and dull, or he prides himself upon his shrewdness and cleverness, and it is, according to all experience that I have been able to gather, most frequently through this avenue that we must gain access to him, the point where we must make the breach to scale his stronghold. Show first of all to the convict, that, adopting his terms, he acts after all foolishly—foolishly according to his own desires. If you omit this, you gain nothing over him. On no one is the mere glow of devotion more absolutely lost than upon the majority of convicts. It is "private, personal and oral instruction" that is wanted. If I said experience has taught me this, I meant my own observation, that of all prison-keepers, and the opinion of intelligent convicts themselves. I relate the following anecdote, not to prove anything, but to illustrate. I have it from sources which admit of no question. A gentleman who visits with great regularity the Philadelphia penitentiary, the inmates of which, his piety prompts him to instruct, had given a bible to a convict, who would ask him, at each visit, with much shrewdness, some difficult question, formed from passages of the bible, each time declaring he would not go on, if this was not first explained to him. The gentleman was unable to persuade him that it would be best for him first to dwell upon those passages which he could easily understand and which palpably applied to him and his situation. After many fruitless trials to induce the convict to this course, his friendly teacher said: "What would you think of a very hungry man, who had not eaten a morcel of food for the last twenty-four hours, and was asked by a charitable man to come in and sit down at a richly covered table, on which there were large dishes of fine meat and also covered ones, the contents of which the hungry man did not know. Instead of satisfying his exhausted body with the former, he lifts one cover after the other, and insists on finding out of what these dishes, unknown to him, are composed. In spite of all the advice of the charitable man to partake first of the more substantial dishes, he dwells with obstinate inquiry on the nicer compounds, until, overcome by exhaustion, he drops down. What would you think of such a man?" "He was a fool," said the convict, "and I will be one no longer. I understand you well."

I was once forcibly struck by the truth, that convicts require careful management. When a prisoner who had asked for a bible—as most of them do after they have been a short time in solitude—and who had received a new testament, promptly demanded the old. On being asked why, he said: "because it is funnier than the new testament."

It is very possible, I think probable, that an organ so placed that all prisoners can hear it, which could be done with perfect ease in our penitentiaries, might have a salutary effect, if hymns and other solemn or otherwise pure music were played. We have never pretended that our penitentiaries are absolutely perfect, nor that the system allows of no farther development: all we contend for is the principle. Music has a wonderfully softening effect; on the rudest sometimes a peculiarly strong effect; it bends the nerves, and renders mild. I know most of my valued Quaker friends will differ from me on this point. No matter; such things may be discussed, may be tried; nay, may leave persons always divided. I am no sentimentalist, and know that sentimentalism in penology is, in its effects, cruel towards the offender as well as society; yet I have always thought, that, on strictly practical grounds, the cultivation of flowers might be introduced in penitentiaries by way of reward; for instance, for rapidly learning to read. A few seeds to be sown in the yard would be a powerful means, and aid in softening, humanizing. We know from history that man remains rude until he begins to till the ground and offer to his gods the first flowers and fruits instead of reeking animals. Why should not the same process repeat itself in the individual? The cultivation of flowers, if unconnected with mere fashion and vanity, cannot but have a softening influence upon the heart, for it makes us take an interest in the silent processes of nature; in her infinite beauties; leads us to observe the minute, and to find pleasure in that which is neither boisterous nor connected with any sacrifice of others. Mr. Mettermayer, the distinguished German criminalist and President of the Chamber of Representatives of Baden, says, in his report on the French bagnes, when they contained the worst population in close contamination, that he found a little flower garden on one of the decks of the hulls, cultivated by the well-behaving convicts in their hours of rest, and that the keeper told him he thought it had a very good effect. Thus many improvements will be made, adaptations to each age will take place, but the principle will remain.

As to *public* worship I repeat, we are opposed to it on principle. I doubt not but now and then a convict would derive benefit from it, but what benefit compared to his having been seen by others and riveted to the horrid chain which unites the criminals. We are cruel by thus exposing the convict. There are many things which might have a good effect upon some. A peaceful evening landscape, a bright moonlight, the sight of happy and industrious reapers, carrying home the produce of their honest labor, might have good effects upon some, but we cannot for all that lead the convicts to enjoy these cheering or imposing views. Can honest and free men have all they know to be beneficial for them?

Permit me to copy a passage of a late pamphlet, written with much practical knowledge of the subject-matter, and drawn up in that spirit of manly love of truth which may well serve as an example for all discussions on this matter. The judicious author says:*

"Ask the gentlemen to whom we just now referred—*Mr. Wiltse*, who superintends the Sing-Sing prison at Mount Pleasant, and Captain Lyndes, who commenced that establishment in an open field, with a detachment of Auburn prisoners as his laborers, and whose opportunities to know the views and habits of such men, few have enjoyed. These gentlemen, and many others within the circle of our acquaintance, will admit, that when the principles of the gospel are brought to bear fairly on the character of a wicked man, (in prison or out of it,) a foundation for reform is secured, in which we may safely confide. But they say, in the same breath, that he who is employed to enforce these principles, and explain them, must possess far more than ordinary acquaintance with the workings of human depravity;—must know well the ground he occupies, and must be wise to win the confidence of those he would teach. They will say, that to send a man among them to preach his two sermons a week, or to ply the prisoners with common-place exhortations to believe and obey what they contemn and hate; or to send to them men of ordinary attainments in piety and religious knowledge, is worse than useless. Whatever pretensions may be made, and however deep and general may be the momentary excitement which it is easy to produce in such ignorant and unoccupied minds, there will be found few, if any, permanent, radical changes of character. The directors of the new Ohio penitentiary at Columbus, in urging upon the legislature the appointment of a permanent chaplain, speak of his labors out of the desk, as fully equal in importance to those in it. 'By visiting the prisoner in the solitude of his cell; making himself acquainted with the structure of his mind, his train of thought, his peculiar propensities, and the degree of moral culture he has heretofore received, he

* Letters on the Comparative Merits of the Pennsylvania and New York Systems of Penitentiary Discipline. By a Massachusetts Man. Boston: 1836. Page 15 and seq.

would do more towards the reformation of the prisoner than by his sermons on the sabbath. In this way he would sometimes find a secret avenue to the heart, through which wholesome counsel and instruction could be conveyed to a prisoner, upon whom a sermon addressed to the multitude would take no effect.'*

"'We should be glad to know when the opportunities for such intercourse occur under the Auburn system, in its best modifications. We have asked the wardens of three of the most important of them, and they admit that they occur *only* at the close of the day, after the prisoner has laid down to rest from his severe labor, and on the sabbath, when the exercises of the chapel, if adapted to their circumstances, would be abundant oral instruction for the day. In regard to the Auburn prison, we have the testimony of a most intelligent and unimpeachable witness, who was on the spot about two years since, and who thus speaks:

" 'The moral improvement of the convicts has never been adequately appreciated. For some time after the present plans were in operation, there was no chaplain; and *religious instruction was considered unfavorable to the maintenance of discipline.* At present, a school is held on Sunday morning, for about two hours, for the purpose of teaching a select number of the most ignorant to read. Divine service is then performed before all the prisoners; after which they are confined in their cells for the remainder of the day. In the afternoon the chaplain visits a few of the cells, this being the only part of the week in which he can confer individually with the prisoners. If such private interviews with the prisoners on week-days be not formally prohibited, (which I believe to be the case,) the practice of holding them is certainly not encouraged, nor does it prevail. The chaplain assured me, that having as many as 680 convicts under his charge, he could not, with every exertion, complete the task of visiting them, going from cell to cell, under a period of three months. Is it reasonable

* Journal of the Legislature of Ohio, 1834–5, p. 74.

to suppose, that services thus restricted, can make any deep impression upon hardened characters such as are the inmates of this prison?"*

"Under the *Pennsylvania system*, opportunities for the fullest intercourse occur without intermission, during the whole day, and part of the evening, all the year round.

"We maintain then, that so far as the religious improvement of the prisoners or the establishment of a religious character is concerned, very little is to be expected from the ordinary preaching of the gospel in prisons, in whatever form the inmates may be assembled. Every thing in their character, situation, manner of attendance and state of mind, is decidedly unfavorable to the just influence of the truth; and if these difficulties were obviated, it requires a much higher degree of intelligence, sagacity, and knowledge of human nature, to approach successfully, men of this class, than is commonly possessed by those to whom this service is assigned. We do not say there are no exceptions to this remark.

"In the view we have taken of the case, thus far, it is a question of little importance, comparatively, whether the *Pennsylvania* or the *Auburn* system affords the greatest facilities for the preaching of the gospel on the sabbath;—for we maintain, that the communication of religious knowledge to men of this class by sermons and exhortations, is unsuited, so far as form and manner are concerned, to their character and circumstances; and even if the present manner were unobjectionable, still the nearer we could come to a system of private, personal teaching, the better; and hence we regard it as a peculiar excellence of the Pennsylvania system, that it permits the truth to be spoken to forty or even seventy individuals at once, *each one of whom is alone.*

"The simple truths of our holy religion fall on the prisoner's ear in the solitude of his cell. This is the nearest approach that is practicable perhaps to that most successful and effectual of all the modes that have ever been tried—*private, personal, oral instruction.*

* Crawford's Report, p. 18.

"In the great assembly, the tear of penitence and the sigh of a broken heart are suppressed by the reproachful frown or the contemptuous sneer of others. But the prisoner in his solitude feels no such restraint. His thoughts are undistracted by the presence of others. He will gain nothing by the demure look or the forced tear of the hypocrite, and the moment the voice of instruction dies upon his ear, *he is alone with God*, and every thing invites to the posture and the language of the returning prodigal.

"For ourselves, we can testify from the experience of many years in this particular department of religious instruction, that the system of discipline adopted in the Eastern penitentiary in Philadelphia, is decidedly more favorable, *on the whole*, to the religious education of the prisoners, than that of any prison on the Auburn plan north of the Potomac."

I have not seen a specific charge against our system on the ground of promoting, more than other systems, a vice of peculiar vileness. In old prisons it is acknowledged to be one of the most frightful evils. It exists likewise in our penitentiaries, both on the Auburn and Pennsylvania plan. It cannot be otherwise, if we consider the debauched life which most convicts have led; nor is it a subject on which we can possibly have very distinct *data*. Certain it seems to me that the vice exists to no greater extent in our penitentiaries than in the Auburn institutions, and, I am inclined to believe, less so. The convict with us can easier be reasoned with, because the warden or minister can converse with him entirely separate from all others; he has always his labor with him and is not idle, and he knows that at any moment the keeper may see him. At any rate, insulation, whether on the Auburn or Pennsylvania plan, prevents a still more disgusting and unnatural vice.

The charge of great expense, I have already met, and nothing more remains now than to give our reasons against the Auburn system, which I shall endeavor to do as briefly as I possibly can, seeing to what extent my letter has already grown.

The advocates of uninterrupted confinement at labor, ready

to acknowledge that the Auburn system is a great improvement upon the old physically and morally filthy mode of imprisonment, because it removes, in a considerable degree, the danger of contamination, makes a greater degree of cleanliness possible, introduces a spirit of order into the prison, teaches the idle to work, keeps the prisoners more healthy and saves the state a great item in the "budget of crime," are nevertheless opposed to it on the following grounds:

1. The Auburn system acknowledges with us, insulation as the fundamental principle of all sound prison discipline, which is not sufficient, indeed, to constitute it, but without which none is possible; but it does not carry through this vital principle; it stops short of its true effect. The convict in an Auburn penitentiary is kept at night in a solitary cell, which, however, does not make it physically impossible to commune with his neighbors; the prisoner, therefore, must be strictly watched. At day the inmates are jointly engaged in large numbers at different sorts of labor, e. g. smithery, cooperage, stone-blasting and cutting, &c. They are strictly watched and must not converse with one another, else they are severely punished; they are not even allowed to take their eyes from the work before them. It is said they do not talk. That they cannot hold long conversations equal in their effect to that frightful degree of contamination which infests the old prisons, where criminals of all sorts are huddled together without labor, or, if with labor, by no means prevented from free intercourse, will be readily admitted. Still we say they do talk, and in a degree which is dangerous, both as to farther contamination, and inasmuch as it prevents that state of calm resignation, which alone can be obtained by uninterrupted solitude, and without which no deep-rooted and steady reform is possible with nearly all, if not all convicts—men whose whole train of thoughts is to be broken and led into an entirely different channel from that in which it flowed while they pursued their criminal path.

The fact that I have brought no evidence to show that perpetual silence cannot be maintained at Auburn, in my translation of the work of Messrs. Beaumont and Tocqueville, though I made sundry notes to it, has been mentioned as tending to corroborate the assertion that perfect silence actually is maintained. If my individual opinion can be of any weight, I will readily state it. I am convinced that the prisoners in Auburn penitentiaries do commune with each other. My conviction is founded upon my personal experience, upon the statement of wardens and chaplains of Auburn prisons, and upon the admission of every former inmate of one of those penitentiaries.

My own experience is that soldiers, at the very moment they pass in parade before their general, will at times talk, and yet neither the leading lieutenant nor the serjeant close behind need ever perceive it. These are soldiers, who but a quarter of an hour later may talk to one another as much as they like: and what have they to say? Perhaps nothing; but men will talk: utterance, that is exteriorising—if I may make a word—his inner man is half his life. And is it really believed men that have to communicate things of great importance to them, will not feel this urgency, which is a thousand times more intense, more burning, because communication is prohibited, and because it can only be done by stealth? Men, whose mode of life has accustomed them to overcome difficulties by cunning and deceit, should not deceive you here? Human nature cannot be changed. Acknowledge with Charles V., who, after countless sacrifices of human life, after armies and treasures had been spent in vain, confessed to Mary of England, in a letter of advice, that he had lost half his life's exertion because he had thought that he possessed power over human nature.

All wardens and chaplains of Auburn penitentiaries, whom I have asked, have not hesitated one moment to admit, that their prisoners do commune, but, add they, of course to a very limited extent, which cannot be dangerous. But I do believe that it is injurious to the prisoner, though it may not be dangerous to the prison authorities.

Whenever I have spoken on this subject with convicts, they have admitted the fact, with a promptness, as if the contrary were out of question. But lately, I visited, in consequence of the general permission which the inspectors of the Philadelphia penitentiary have given me, a prisoner, a native of America, in his lonely cell. He knew, of course, nothing of my arrival, and the moment I entered he said: "How do you do, Mr. Lieber?" Mr. Lieber! said I, astonished; where have you ever seen me? Prisoner: "Why, sir, did you not visit, some years ago, Sing-Sing?" I did, but how do you know my name? Prisoner: "You asked Mr. Wiltse for a cat, with which we are flogged there, and carried it away, did'nt you?" All this is true, but how do you come to know it? Prisoner: "Oh! as to that, the barber was present when you got the cat; (here he mentioned other details which had appeared interesting to the barber, a fellow-convict)." But how did you come to know all that? Prisoner: "Such things are known in a day or two all over the prison. We pass it along in the lock step." I now made farther inquiry, upon which the prisoner told me, that they receive not unfrequently information from without, through discharged convicts, who leave papers in places fixed upon when they were inmates, and that such information is passed along until it reaches the interested person. He farther told me that they know the names of new-comers, their sentence and offence, and agree on points of rendezvous after discharge. "Do you agree on new schemes?" I inquired; "Not frequently," he said, "except when it can be done with a few words." Now every one knows how easy it is to communicate a considerable train of ideas by mere indications, if we speak to one of our profession on a subject belonging to it, because he reasons as we do, knows our chain of thoughts, and three, four points will be sufficient to construe the whole figure. So do familiar friends understand each other rapidly by a few words in their correspondence; so has the commander to write but a few words to his generals on whole vast positions; so does the nurse understand the few incoherent sounds of the infant.

Our conversation turned farther upon the treatment; his eyes flashed when he spoke of the whip, and said that many a one is innocently whipped because the keeper believes he has seen him talk. He rose to a high degree of passion, and at length he exclaimed: "Sir, that prison makes bitter enemies; we know we cannot ward off being flogged, because it is impossible to avoid the appearance of talking or a smile. I know," he said emphatically, "I am criminal, but we all feel what is right or not." There was a pathos of passion in this man, a degree of bitter indignation, which attracted far more my attention than I am wont to lend to the complaints of prisoners, except they relate to facts which I have it in my power to ascertain; yet I have not related the conversation to speak on this point, but only to show how much credit we are bound to give to the sequel. When this man had spoken himself into actual wrath, I asked: "Do you believe they could master 800 or 1000 criminals without the cat, and without the right in every keeper to lash them on the spot, without previous permission?" "No, never," he exclaimed, without a moment's hesitation, "their throats would soon be cut." It is this confession of a convict in the very moment of ire, kindled by the remembrance of humiliating punishment, which is important. The same convict told me likewise that the prisoners are very greedy to obtain newspapers, old or new, entire or torn; that they often obtain them in boxes which the hatters send back, through the cooks, barbers, or in any other way, and that in spite of all the severe punishment pending over them, they do contrive to hide, read and pass them along.

Another conversation of importance, with a warden of one of the most noted penitentiaries, may find its place here. When I visited, last summer, the Wethersfield penitentiary, where I was received both by the warden and the excellent and judicious chaplain, with great kindness, I asked Mr. Pilsbury whether he thought the two systems were founded on different principles. He answered in the negative, and added that he considered the Pennsylvania system only differing in this, that it carried the distinguishing principle of both, more consistently through. When I asked him whether he had any objection against my making public use of this declaration, coming from a source of so great experience, he assured me that he never had any objection against publicly confessing what was his conviction, and his conviction was what he had stated. I thus have made public use of his permission, and publicly thank him for it.

If we assume it as a fact that communications as indicated above, take place—and I do not see how the fact can be gainsaid—every body of any penologic experience will admit, that they are sufficient to defeat, in a very great degree, the intended effects of insulation. Can that mind be at rest, calm and reflective, which has received the seed of a new appointment for criminal plotting? Can that mind be fit for better thoughts which is racked by curiosity to know who this or that fellow convict is; for what he has been sentenced; where he comes from? Can that prisoner be disposed to allow milder feelings to enter his heart, who burns with daily challenged indignation and is curbed by the surest of all means of curbing, fear of bodily pain?

2. We object to the Auburn system on the ground to which I have already alluded, namely, the violence which it absolutely requires. Either you make people who are congregated keep silence or you do not. If not, you abandon the principle of insulation; if you do, you must use as violent means as it would require to keep the hungry from seizing upon victuals before them. Nature cannot be counteracted by mild means. The desire, the urgent want of communion, without reference to the subject of communion, is an inmost and original longing, a vital instinct of our organization. Without it mankind would not be mankind. I found once a prisoner in the Philadelphia penitentiary who told me that it was music to his ears to hear the shuttle of his neighbor, and that without knowing who he was, he used to vie with him in the swiftness of using it. I heard once, in visiting a cell, an indistinct knock against the wall, which came from the next cell. I asked what it was; who was the neighbor? The prisoner answered that he did not know, as was the fact, but that once and a while his neighbor knocked and he answered. And for what purpose, I inquired; is it a sign? No sir, he replied; of what should we

give signs? It is only that he says, here am I, and I answer, I am here. The prisoner would have expressed his idea more distinctly had he said: "My neighbor says, here is a man; and I answer, a man is here." He owned he had been told not to do it, and it was always at the risk of the keeper's hearing it; still they did it now and then. So urgent is the abstract desire of communion, so irksome it is "to be alone;" and we are expected to believe that men seeing each other, working close to each other, marching in actual contact with each other, the mouth of one close to the ear of the other, do not talk!

We do not blame the keepers of the Auburn penitentiaries for using the whip; they must do it. Let us hear nothing about the possibility of carrying on those prisons without flogging on the spot. The respective wardens must know it best, and they all insist upon the necessity. Ask them if they would dare to remain warden one hour after the right of flogging had been taken from them. It is for this very necessity of the whip that we declare the system itself objectionable; because the whip degrades, irritates, exasperates, not to speak of the frequent abuse which must take place and does take place, for prison keepers are but men. Do you believe a man of some education will make up his mind to live peacefully and strive to regain the favor of society, who knows and indelibly feels that he has been flogged in presence of fifty or a hundred convicts? Who does, I fear does not know human nature.

3. The inmate of an Auburn penitentiary becomes known by sight to a vast community of criminals, who, by their very life of crime, disperse in all directions. Whoever has been an inmate of an Auburn prison must fear at every step to meet with an acquaintance, to be exposed, to see his possible endeavors to live honestly frustrated, except he have a degree of moral fortitude which we cannot expect; his offence is the very evidence of this want. I have seen young men of decent and some of high-standing families, working in common with the other criminals at Sing-Sing. It is right that there be not a different punishment for the rich or the poor: but if justice demands that the poorest emigrant should not be treated harsher

than the son of a fashionable family, justice likewise demands that you should not throw an additional and immensely weighty punishment upon the latter. He is gazed at by the visiters in his unfortunate dress, among fellow-felons; and can you believe he will meekly bend down and say: "all, all is just?" The Auburn system, then, does not furnish an accommodable punishment.

4. It is absolutely necessary that the community should have confidence in a prison. This can only be maintained by free access to it, either of every one who chooses to go, or of persons in whom the public repose confidence—properly elected inspectors. Yet every visiter gazing at the prisoner, when in common with others, is a new thrust at him which removes him farther from society. Visits ought to be allowed but to very few indeed, and then made to the single prisoner, which cannot be the case in Auburn prisons. Still more objectionable is the permission given to females to visit the prison, as is the case, for instance in Charlestown. It ought never to be done.

5. Finally, it is impossible, if the principle of cheapness shall be preserved, to give to the cells on the Auburn plan those dimensions and that character which are requisite, not to effect a feeling of comfort, but of calmness, without which the prisoner must grow worse and worse. Penned up in a very narrow cell, gloomy and every way striking the mind of the prisoner with the horrid reality that he is debased; that the man in him is not appealed to, he cannot be expected to soften in thought and feeling.

We think, then, that the Auburn system does not effect what it strives to effect; does not afford an accommodable punishment; does not sufficiently prevent the growing worse of the convict; does not obtain the highest effect with the smallest means; requires physical violence to be maintained, and, therefore, irritates anew; is not well calculated for that religious or intellectual instruction which the criminal requires; does not prevent entirely contamination, and does not calm the prisoner, while it offers no other advantage than that of saving money in the first outlay, which, we think, is vastly overbalanced by the steady, sure, mild, yet effective mode of the Pennsylvania system, and therefore believe the latter to be greatly preferable.

I cannot conclude this letter without confessing that it is painful to me to observe that very rarely a distinction is made in the discussions on this subject of momentous interest, between the prison systems and the respective penitentiaries. Real or supposed defects of our penitentiaries have been attacked in discussions on the merits of solitary confinement. If these defects exist, by all means expose them, though before you make the charge be convinced of their existence. But what has this to do with the system? If the prisoners in the Eastern Penitentiary really could commune with each other it would be bad, but it changes nothing as to the system, for no one will deny that it is within the sphere of human power to build cells, between which all communication can be prevented.

In having thus, Sir, expressed my opinion, you will feel convinced that I have stated what I hold to be true after long and repeated observation. When I came to this country many years ago, I knew nothing of the merits of either system. My attention was first drawn to the Auburn penitentiaries. I was struck with their great superiority over other prisons: when I became acquainted, however, with the Pennsylvania system, it appeared to me superior, and every year's observation of both systems, as well as my reading on the subject, have confirmed my opinion more and more. I have no personal interest in the matter, not even one that might influence me unconsciously. Unconnected with any man of note on one or the other side, I have invariably been kindly received by the wardens of all penitentiaries, whenever I have paid them visits, which I hope to repeat yet many times. I have stated what I believe, and why I believe it—a right which every citizen possesses, and the exercise of which must be ever welcome to all who love truth, for by the exchange of ideas alone a cause can gain. Verily, the prisoners do not exist for the penitentiaries, nor have we to defend one or the other system because it is that or the other. If it is difficult to acknowledge that as error, for which we have long conscientiously spoken, written and acted, and especially, if it so should happen that we have committed indiscretions in defending it, let us nevertheless be men and own our errors. What is it to mankind, to the cause of humanity; what to the broad current of civilization which rolls from century to century, whether that system which finally shall prevail, has this or that name, originated here or there? What, before all, matters it to the unfortunate, helpless, crime-stricken fellow-man, whether one or the other name should prevail? Let us think of his crime, of the grave subject we profess to be interested in for him, for society, for civilization; think of it like men, and cast away small vanity, which will be forgotten and buried in utter oblivion, within the space of a few years, while for centuries to come one or the other system will prevail for the honor of mankind, which had the power over those who offended, violated and provoked, yet which used that power so far as true wisdom and kindness demanded it, and no farther.

I own I have not always been able to suppress the suspicion, that the discussions on the respective merits of the two disciplinary systems have not remained untainted by feelings which stand in no connexion with the essential character of the discipline advocated or attacked, but rather with the places where they originated. If this be the case it would be well to change the names of Pennsylvania and Auburn systems, which besides are not scientific, while the stricter terms—uninterrupted confinement at labor, and the still more unwieldy one which designates the character of the Auburn systems, are too long for common use.* No one can like better than myself, historical

* Confinement may be classified thus: It is either joint confinement (as in the old prisons) or choristic confinement, (founded on separation; in Greek *chorisis.*) The latter may be eremitic confinement, (from *eremit,* from the

reminiscences carried along in the names of things; they have to me generally a deeper meaning than strictly scientific terms. Yet a man must be very superficially acquainted with history, not to know the difficulties, heart-burning and suffering which have been caused by names and obstinate adherence to them. We ought to have learnt at least so much of the grave lessons which history gives on every page, as willingly to cast off names, whenever they seem to offer serious difficulties. Let us labor and struggle for things and not for sounds. A man must know little of mankind if by this time he has not yet learnt, that all civilized communities stand in need of all. If the Phenician brings the letters to Greece, shall the Greek refuse them because a Phenician brought them?

I had concluded and signed this letter, when I received the papers which contain the royal speech at the late opening of the French chambers. I congratulate you, myself, every friend of man, on a passage in that document, which I cannot refrain from adding as a cheering postscript: "Our penitentiary system has long called for all the attention of my government, and you will have to examine a bill for its improvement."

It is not that Louis Philippe has pronounced it, which is so pleasing to the advocate of prison reform: who would not expect such views of a good and honest man? It is not that a king has said it: what is that to us? I rejoice at the fact that there it stands in a throne-speech, which is to be considered as the sum total of that which, after much reflection, weighing,

---

eremia, solitude,) by which every prisoner is absolutely separated from the others, or it may be silential confinement, in which he is separated by silence. The word silentiary has been used already. Eremitic for the Auburn system is certainly correct; we want to make, for the time, eremits of them, that they may be severed from the world, and become contemplative. If silential is not so well sounding a word, I own I cannot find a better one. Terms designating the same and derived from the Greek, siopatic would be still more out of place. I hope I may not be charged with tarrying too long with names; it is the very difficulty caused by names which I am desirous of removing.

remodelling and correction the chief organs of one party, at least, and of the power of the state have found indispensably necessary to say, not to their party, but to the nation; it is at least that which appears highly important to the most powerful party, modified by a regard to the views of all others—the product of the national view at the time, when it touches matters which cannot in their nature, serve as ministerial hook and bait. How long is it since Beccaria and Howard dared to represent the criminal as an unfortunate man, who, though criminal, still remains a man, and to tell mankind that their penal codes and punishments were cruel and unwise? Hardly half a century has elapsed, and here the principle has worked itself already into a crown speech, not into an insulated law, which may or not effect good—no, it is treated as a great national question of a country which counts thirty-four millions of inhabitants. Howard was laughed at, Romilly was treated with contempt, for troubling their minds with so mean a subject as criminals in prison; and here, after so brief a period, the king of one of the vastest nations on earth is caused by all-powerful public opinion to recapitulate it, condensed and distinct, from the pinnacle of the national fabric, in favor of prison reform. Let us contemplate for a moment how slow, how very slow great thoughts and good principles travelled and expanded in former times. Early enough, centuries ago, it was pronounced by great minds that public schools are one of the chief agents and supporters of civilization. Charlemagne knew it, said it, acted on it; and since, when has the principle been acted out on a large and efficient scale? The noble period is approaching when neither glory or financial dispositions alone, nor matters of utilitarianism alone—which, if taken in mere materialism, is the barbarism of our times, and each age has its own—shall furnish the topics for crown speeches or governors' messages; but when glory, patriotism, utility and subjects of deep humanity, of ethic and intellectual worth, purely scientific enterprises and elevating arts—all, all that is good and noble and ennobling shall be matters of broad national concern—of real life and action, and not only of a few sages or solitary priests of humanity and civilization. The wine works; let us be of good cheer.

With high regard,

Dear Sir,

Your obedient servant,

FRANCIS LIEBER.

Columbia, S. C., January 1838.

ERRATA.

The reader is requested to correct the following errors of the press, which escaped correction in consequence of the absence of the author from Philadelphia.

Page 8, line 30th from the top, for course read *source*.
10, line 4th ,, ,, allow read *allows*.
11, line 35th ,, ,, state of political action read *political action of the state*.
13, line 2nd ,, ,, chains, war, read *chasing war*.
—, line 23d ,, ,, after punish strike out semi-colon and insert *comma*.
14, line 18th ,, ,, for but read *best*.
16, line 23d ,, ,, aggravation read *its gradation*.
20, line 23d ,, ,, because it is opposition, but because the opposition leads to evils, read *because the opposition leads to evils, but because it is opposition*.
21, line 24th from the top, for those read *that*.
23, line 9th ,, ,, offence read *offender*.
24, line 3d ,, ,, as rational and moral beings, read *as a rational and moral being*.
—, line 28th ,, ,, strike out *moreover*.
25, line 6th ,, ,, for and read *it*.
29, line 7th ,, ,, strike out *once*.
32, line 21st ,, ,, after destroyed strike out the period and insert a *colon*.
42, line 31st ,, ,, for variety read *society*.
44, line 38th ,, ,, after Apology insert *or*.
49, line 2nd ,, ,, for it read *reform*.
54, line 23d ,, ,, coast read *court*.
55, line 30th ,, ,, insert comma after sentenced.
64, line 16th ,, ,, for night read *sight*.
75, last line, for individuals read *convicts*.
76, line 6th, from the top, for cares read *cases*.
91, last line, insert *Greek* after the, at the end of the line.
92, line 30th, from the top, for Auburn read *Pennsylvania*.
93, line 17th ,, ,, their minds read *his mind*.

Made in the USA
Monee, IL
04 November 2026

67388644R00056